WIRED
GOD IN YOU

By Craig Smee

FOREWARD BY
Daniel Amstutz, Mark Welch and Tafara Butayi

EDITED BY
Jeanne Menendez

NIMBLE.CHURCH
A UTurn Ministry Project
www.nimble.church

NIMBLE.CHURCH
Wired – God In You
By Craig Smee

Copyright © 2016 by Nimble.Church

Requests for information should be addressed to info@nimble.church

Unless otherwise specified, all scriptures from the New Living Translation or the New King James Version.

All rights reserved. No part of this publication may be reproduced, stored in a retrieval system, or transmitted in any form or by any means – electronic, mechanical, photocopy, recording, or any other – except for brief quotations in printed reviews, without the prior permission of the publisher and author.

ISBN-13: 9781521374429
ASIN: B01FVH1EYC

DEDICATION

To the Father, Son and Holy Spirit

To my incredible wife Leanne and my amazing children; Kevin, Bianca and Kyle. You prove God's love is real.

WHAT'S IN WIRED?

"LOOK – SQUIRREL"	1
"I LOVE IT WHEN A PLAN COMES TOGETHER"	21
GRAVITY RULES	35
MIRROR MIRROR	47
KNOW, NOW DO	59
UNWRAPPED	69
BLIND FAITH	79
BLESSED	91
TRUE NORTH	105
PHOTO ALBUM	117
THE END OF IT ALL	129
ABOUT THE AUTHOR	145

ACKNOWLEDGMENTS

To an incredible mother-in-law and father-in-law—Alec and Colleen you prayed me right—thank you.

Jeanne—You took the time to transform my words into something readable—thank you.

Thank you to those leaders and pastors who so graciously contributed to this book and to my journey.

PREFACE

In the search to make sense of some of life's most basic questions, humankind has lost touch with where we came from and who we really are. Discover some principles that have been part of the race to be human since before time—divine principles that became part of our DNA template, wired into us at creation. <u>Wired</u> takes a real look at our relationship with God, our belief, faith and ability to walk through life despite some of its difficulties. Craig Smee was brought up in a religious world that caused hurt and rebellion. Having to rebuild his life from the bottom up, he looks at Christianity and God from a perspective that is fresh and unique all the while staying true to scripture.

Craig is a husband to a beautiful God loving wife, a father to three incredible followers of Jesus, has planted several churches, led at a high level in corporate organizations, is a respected speaker and a social and digital media apostle. Above all Craig is well qualified to write on changing life around for the better—he has had to do it himself.

FOREWARD
COMMENTS BY OTHERS

DANIEL AMSTUTZ
DEAN OF WORSHIP & ARTS AT CHARIS BIBLE COLLEGE, WOODLAND PARK, COLORADO

I am honored to recommend this timely book in an age when identities are being stolen and destroyed every day! Discover how you've been "Wired" by God Himself and the resulting freedom in His love for you! Knowing where you've come from will help you know where you're going! This book will encourage you to discover God's ability IN YOU, through Christ, resulting in transformation that is limitless..... and timely! Open your heart to the promises of God and learn the rhythm of grace!

MARK WELCH
LEAD PASTOR OF THE POINTE CHURCH ANTELOPE, CALIFORNIA

If you struggle with your identity, Wired by Craig Smee is for you. Since my beginnings in pastoral ministry in 1982, I have counseled hundreds of teens, and men and women of all ages, who are caught in a seemingly never-ending loop of sin and behavior issues. So many times, the idea that they were made for higher purposes and to live a life of victory seems to elude those in this predicament. Is there a way for them to discover why they are here?

One of my counseling experiences was in the spring of 1989, in my pastor's office in Moncton, New Brunswick, Canada. I was meeting with a French Canadian named Jean (John) who had attended a large community Easter program our church had sponsored and I had directed.

I listened as Jean shared his life's story. He had grown up in Quebec, Canada, in a devoutly religious home. To be French Canadian to him was synonymous with the religion he had been raised in. "I am French Canadian so I am a _____," he said (you can fill in your own blank based on your background).

And yet Jean was empty. There was a God-shaped place in his heart that could not be filled with religion, with philosophy, or with any other pursuit. In his desperate attempt to fill his emptiness he had tried all manner of things, from money to substances. Nothing worked. Now he sat in my office seeking satisfaction and meaning. As we talked and I shared how Christ came to make him right with God, the lights began to come on. "Just as soon as I clean myself up," Jean said, "I will give my life to Jesus."

Jean is like so many others, who somehow cannot imagine God would care about them the way they are. He felt unworthy and unclean. He imagined God would rather judge him and cast him out forever than to ever want him near. Fortunately for Jean, he listened to the words of Christ that day. He came to understand that he had been "wired" to have a relationship with God, and that if he only came as he was, God would receive him. He believed and received God's immeasurable gift of grace. His life, and that of his family and countless others changed because of the radical way God restored him to what he was made to be. Jean himself became a pastor and a chaplain, and enjoyed the last year of his life in the "joy" of his maker.

That is the message of this book. Craig Smee takes his years of personal and pastoral experience and opens up in ways that most writers and pastors would never do. He digs in deep to the root cause of so many people's spiritual issues and vices—their spiritual identity conflict.

Craig, like my friend Jean, came to a place where he was desperate for connection with God and starving for a sense of purpose. And he found it! Now he is sharing this message with the world in this amazing writing.

I recommend that you sit down, say a prayer in the best way you know and tell God you desire to know who He is so you can discover who He made you to be. And get ready to go on a journey of God-discovery, which will lead to self-discovery like you may have never experienced. God bless you as you read and discover Wired.

TAFARA BUTAYI
AUTHOR AND LEAD PASTOR OF FAITH HILL CHURCH, JOHANNESBURG SOUTH AFRICA

My good friend Craig has penned a great book that will challenge, excite and at the same time encourage you. Wired is a photography of what a Christian life entails - get ready to be blessed.

INTRODUCTION

WIRED – GOD IN YOU

Thank you for choosing to read Wired. This book is dedicated to honoring God and seeking who He has made you to be.

I truly hope that this book will help you find practical application to basic core scriptural principles that have been so deeply wired into you by God Himself. I hope that my ramblings will stir in you a real desire to just pick up your Bible again and for you to start passionately living the Word. I hope that it will help you get to know God in a personal and intimate way, and that it will ignite a truly inspiring relationship with your heavenly Father: one that He desires to have with you.

I have been a pastor for over twelve years, which is a relatively short time compared to some of the incredibly faithful men that have helped shape my ministry. So, probably like many pastors, I will say what I think should be said with the utopian belief that it will in fact change the world. I fully appreciate my humor is humorless and my academic rhetoric is sometimes pointless. My friends think my jokes are corny and you are not alone if you feel concern for the ministries in which I hold a leadership role.

I wrote this book with an intense passion for people. I have a deep-seated longing to watch people who are living mediocre Christian lives find some real hardcore passion and start being radical Christians, either again or for the first time, once they really get to know the God who is overflowing with love for them.

Too many Christians have huge impact potential, but either aren't aware of it or opt to sit back and do nothing with it. Every now and then, they have a discussion or an experience that temporarily gets them excited for life, God or both. Recognizing a person's undiscovered and undefined potential drives me to the point of Holy Discontent. Have you heard it said of you that "you have so much potential?" I don't know about you, but I want to be "successful" for the rest of my life, not just full of "potential."

People all over the world are seeking God. They need more and want more from Him but have missed the basics of how to experience His passion and love. For the most part, they have judged Him and the church and by so doing have distanced themselves from the One true source of passion and blessing. Once we understand the basic principles of who He is, His love begins to fill in that gnawing gap that exists in the lives of people who don't know Him.

A few years ago a pipe burst at our home and flooded our swimming pool. The sand that washed into the pool clogged up everything. It took us weeks to clean the filters and get the pump back on track. That experience made me think of so many people I know whose lives are bogged down and clogged up with everything else that life throws at them when they are really keen to be something for God. Most of the time, people knowingly and willingly seem to choose to stay clogged up rather than to flow in the freedom that our loving God makes available to us when we get to know Him. Some, on the other hand, don't know where to start in the process of unclogging their thinking and aligning themselves to God again.

In John 8:32, we are told that "the truth will set you free." God passionately desires for you to be free. So in this book you will find some hard truths, mostly about who God is and who He sees you to be. Hopefully these biblical truths will help you to want to find your freedom, to define your personal abilities and will teach you how you can practically achieve the freedom that God wants you to have.

Love, trust, obedience and blessings, make sense to me. They have created a passion in me that has helped me work towards my Spiritual potential. Hopefully this book will help you on your way to finding your freedom in God's love. I truly pray that as you journey to a greater appreciation of the Creator's love, that it will inspire in you a trust that compels you to be obedient to Him. As a result of your obedience, I know you will step into a place of blessings for your life.

CHAPTER ONE
"LOOK – SQUIRREL"

The grass withers, the flower fades, Because the breath of the Lord blows upon it; Surely the people are grass. The grass withers, the flower fades, But the word of our God stands forever." – Isaiah 40:7,8

On my grade one report card, my teacher, Mrs. Dolman, wrote that "Craig needs to focus more and not get so easily distracted." Back then (my daughter would tell you that it was a very long time ago) we did not have all the acronyms and abbreviations for that kind of behavior that we have today. But even today I am easily distracted and much prefer to start things and not have to worry about the details of finishing them.

We live in a world that is bent on distracting us and sadly that has become part of our spiritual journey and relationship with God. And if the distractions of the world are not enough, we have an incredible ability to create them, come up with excuses or just procrastinate getting things done.

We even get distracted within our belief structures, church life and relationship with God. I call it "doctrinal distraction." There are so many tools available these days that it is often difficult to know where to begin in our attempts to pull ourselves from a spiritual slump or to find the necessary motivation to push through the tough times.

When money is tight should I read a book on prosperity or stewardship? When children are not listening, should I dive into a book on discipline or relationships? When marriage is the worst thing in my life, should I bury myself in a book on getting through divorce or one on submission?

So many Christians seem to exhibit an insatiable hunger to find the one devotional or one power phrase that will complete their Christian "quest" and make sense of their journey with God. Just as they feel they have found it, something happens that seems to make no sense and the quest begins again. In the process they miss some basic divine truths; truths that hold the key to solving both individual challenges and global problems. Truths that God Himself has wired into every one of us.

As individuals running in this sometimes seemingly endless hamster wheel of faith versus reality versus the self-help book we are currently reading, we begin to shape churches around how we feel, manufacture scripture that makes sense and create a journal of man-made doctrines. We find a set of activities that seems to fill our God need. These activities become our world; and then when we meet others who don't agree with our activities or have activities of their own that seem to fulfill them, we plant another church, give it a new mission statement and start the whole process over again: a process that is far from God and His principles and one that can easily be called religion.

The church cannot fulfill her destiny as the hope of the world if her individual members cannot grasp and practice life based on the basic principles of the God whom they claim to serve.

Our easily distracted mind, the self-oriented answers we offer or the abundant resources available are not the real problems. We have developed into a society that does not focus, study through and discover God's principles for themselves. Like my first grade report card said, we "need to focus more and not get so easily distracted." We seldom delve deeper than a feel good read or a temporary motivation.

But there is still a place where we can find out who God is and how He genuinely feels about us. There is a place that we can discover principles that have been put in place for our benefit that not even God would change. Principles that were so wise in their creation that they stand for all time. These principles were placed in us so that we could gain a sense of completion and wholeness. When we deviate from them we find ourselves in turmoil and disconnected from the peace that we were designed to enjoy. Scripture is the story of mankind wrestling with these principles and working through them. Scripture is not a set of rules and regulations, or even a set of principles imposed upon us. Scripture is God letting us know how he wired us and what principles were molded into who we are.

> *All Scripture is given by inspiration of God, and is profitable for doctrine, for reproof, for correction, for instruction in righteousness, that the man of God may be* **complete,** *thoroughly equipped for every good work. - 2 Timothy 3:16-17 (emphasis mine)*

We are made complete when we turn to scripture to find the answers, direction and the vision that we desire. Scripture connects what we know about God to what we know about ourselves. Rarely do we find a book that is able to completely revolutionize a community, that can directly highlight the error of our ways and passionately give us fulfillment and not fear: a book that, with some study, meditation and application, changes our lives so radically. But it's not just the Bible that can change our hearts. We need to have a full revelation and understanding of who God is, how he sees us and how He has wired us to be. Otherwise we get right back to our search for the quick fix, and we will use the Bible to find scriptures or quotations to simply give us momentary answers to immediate problems or that temporarily fills some gap in our lives.

If God is to work powerfully and constantly in our lives, He is not only interested in the singular and isolated issues that we expect Him to solve, but He is concerned with our complete spiritual being, the complexity of who we are and who we are becoming. He loves the challenge of not just fixing the immediate problem—the miracles—but also finding a chain reaction of events that will constantly propel us into greatness and eternity—the blessing.

He does not just want to remove the pain of a lost loved one, He wants to see an entire family change despite the grief. He does not just want a church to hand out a piece of bread and a cup of soup to a few hungry children in downtown Johannesburg South Africa, He wants to see churches come together and transform the entire city.

He summed up His desire for us to catch the dream, when He asked us to pray "Let Your Kingdom come." He wants us to desire far reaching, long lasting and earth shaking change that shouts out mighty messages of His glory. He does not want us to just settle for the warm feeling of a good read, the momentary motivation of a good sermon or the brief sense of belonging through the scheduled program of the local church.

God is a global healer. His touch is thorough, deep and complete and leaves no part of us unaffected. Our worship of Him and obedience to His ways exposes us to a cause and effect on a Divine scale. A single act of obedience sets off a chain reaction of supernatural interventions in multiple areas of our lives.

I have been blessed to counsel many people and have seen one singular truth that in most cases has unlocked not just a revelation of the immediate solution to a problem, but in keeping with the wholeness of who God is, has reshaped entire lives.

When we begin to understand the principles of who God is, and who He is in us, then we begin to understand that those principles, when implemented, affect every area of our lives, not only through their simplicity, their practicality or their relevance, but also by their total and global effect on our lives and our walk with God.

We can run around like chickens without heads, reading this or watching that in an attempt to grasp what He means, who He is, what He is in us or we can stand tall, firm and triumphant knowing exactly what the Word is saying to us about the God we worship, and we can give our all to unashamedly worshiping him.

The Word is straightforward and true. His Word is constant and global, yet simple and comprehensible. It lasts forever. The plan, as laid out in Scripture, for relationship with God and blessings from Him, never changes. What it asked of servants in the days of Abraham, Isaac and Jacob, it asks of us today. Where Adam and Eve failed, we often fail today. The consequences of ignoring its Truth are as dire today as they were then.

CHAPTER TWO
FREE CHOICE

It is the same with my word. I send it out, and it always produces fruit. It will accomplish all I want it to, and it will prosper everywhere I send it. - Isaiah 55:11

The request that God made of the first human beings and the request He makes of us today is exactly the same. The circumstances under which that request is made, however, are vastly different.

Adam and Eve did not have the complete example of God's plan in the form of Jesus Christ, or the wonderful counsellor and helper in the guidance of the Holy Spirit. Quite frankly, they had no need for them. The lack of sin made Christ's ransom sacrifice unnecessary. The gifts of the Holy Spirit were the order of the day. All they knew was God. All three, all the time. He walked with them, talked to them and shared with them the intimacies of His Being.

It must have been incredible. No question without a complete answer, no explanation devoid of divine wisdom and no situation without an outcome completely wrapped in peace.

God had huge plans for Adam and Eve. They were to be the parents of a blessed race, reproducing children in the image of God. They were to be the founders of a world order of people that would always be positioned in God's blessing.

The human race that would grow from the first couple would all enjoy the same intimate and personal relationship that Adam and Eve enjoyed. God would honor each of them through His gift of free will. Because of the incredible relationship that they would enjoy with the Creator, they would never willfully want to be disobedient to Him. It would make no sense to be disobedient to the One who made them and evidently loved them so much. Just before He took rest, God took a step back to see just how good He had made the world for mankind. He had made everything just right.

Then God saw everything that He had made, and

indeed it was very good. So the evening and the morning were the sixth day. - Genesis 1:31

He gave Adam and Eve every option and every choice that they could ever want. When creating each of them, He replaced animal instinct with the gift of free will. They would have endless choices to make as they grew. They would have complete freedom to make any decision they wanted. Yet every decision they made would be made in the glorious presence, perfect peace and perfect wisdom of God Himself. He made them in His image with the ability to creatively choose their own destiny but had given them every reason to choose His way. He had established them and provided for them.

Obedience in Eden was simple. It was choosing the best way of bringing glory to a Creator who had held nothing back from His creation. All God wanted was for them to choose that way. The multitude of choices they were able to make along the way, would never detract from their primary desire to be obedient to the awesomeness of their Father.

For example, when Adam was choosing a name for the big cat that roared every evening, he could have taken years to come up with the name that suited the animal. A name that suited its looks, or the noises it made or the way it ate its food. Instead every time he chose a name he made the free choice that gave glory to the One who had created it. He must have chatted away with his Creator asking why He had made that specific animal, how He had made it and how it fitted in with the rest of creation. He could have called it anything. He had free choice. But because Adam wanted to give God glory in every decision, no wrong could have come from whatever he decided.

Free will was not a test, but an added testimony to God's desire for His creation, humankind, to make the very best choice. He simply wanted them to choose Him because they loved Him. He did not want them to be wired and programmed to love and obey Him. He wanted them to *choose* to trust Him. He desired that it be their choice to obey Him and thus to receive all the blessings that He had in store for them. Obedience to the principles of God connected who they were wired to be to the One who had wired them.

He wanted every human being who would ever walk the earth to feel the rush of standing before a difficult decision with the optimal, God honoring choice naturally welling up from a deep sense of adoration. That sense of fulfillment, that sense of peace and direction would be the blessing. Their natural, free will obedience would result in blessing.

But that ability to choose was a pretty risky gift from the Creator's point of view. It was potentially the worst thing He could give us. Would it not have been easier and more sensible to just preprogram us to do what He required? Predestine each human to a predetermined set of choices?

The answer to that is found in a well-used and biblical definition of who God is—*God is love*. He is infinite Love. If we choose Him on our own accord, it is the best testimony to the love that He desires of us. If we choose Him because He inspires us, it is the ultimate choice of love. For this reason, He gave us free choice. What love would it be if we were just preprogrammed to love Him?

As a father, I would much prefer my children to voluntarily express their love to me rather than being forced. In the same way, God does not force Himself on us.

The obvious result of free choice exceeds thousands upon millions of possibilities. Every time another DNA string is put together to form another unique human being, another set of unique choices and possible outcomes are born. This is where God's omnipotence and omnipresence become so apparent. This is where the expression "alpha and omega, the beginning and the end" truly comes into its own. We begin to demonstrate these principles of God simply by making decisions. The fact that He has a plan for every one of our choices, as well as every one of the resultant possibilities, demonstrates His incredible presence and His perfect ability. It shows us His divine wisdom and how infinitely deep His grace really runs. Put simply, God is already at the outcome of a decision before we make it.

God had already considered every consequence and outcome that could possibly arise from every choice Adam and Eve could have ever made.

God put a divine plan in place that would ensure the ultimate fulfillment of His will *and* that would take care of any and all of the consequences of free will. He is able to keep His will and purpose as well as the unknown of our free will in complete harmony.

Had Adam sinned and Eve remained faithful, God had a plan. If Eve had fallen and Adam remained faithful, God had a plan. If they had both remained faithful and Cain or Abel succumbed, God in His infinite wisdom had a divine plan.

Adam and Eve could have made any one of thousands of choices on the fateful day that they were visited by the serpent, and God would have been ready for every one.

Obviously God had a preferred choice. There was one option that He knew would bring about the best results. But He would not force them into it. He wanted them to see that their every need and desire would be fulfilled through complete obedience. Yet in His incredible mercy, He would continue to take care of them, even if they did not choose the one singularly optimal way. He would still provide a divine means of correcting a disobedient decision.

*For as by one man's disobedience many were made sinners, so also by one Man's **obedience** many will be made righteous. - Genesis 5:19 (emphasis mine)*

He wanted them to understand that He had already made them aware of the choice that would result in the best possible outcome. If Adam and Eve had chosen the way God recommended, that blessing would have been so far reaching and so complete that it would have taken care of every aspect of human existence. God's plan has not changed.

He does not condemn you for making poor decisions. He does not toss you aside because you were disobedient. He is just looking to restore the blessing in your life that was taken from mankind through the free will choices made in the Garden of Eden.

This is the beginning of understanding of how God has wired Himself into each of us. We have an inherent desire to improve, to grow and make progress. We sometimes make the wrong decisions along the way but we generally pick ourselves up and try again. God wired us like that because He is like that. He always has a plan despite our choices.

We choose God and make decisions that honor Him not because we are programmed that way but because, since the beginning of time, He has always wanted the very best for us. Even when we, just like Adam and Eve, make choices that are not optimum, that do not honor Him, He still comes looking for us.

Then the Lord God called to Adam and said to him, "Where are you?" - Genesis 3:9

The human understanding and definition of obedience has been distorted. When we hear that we have to obey or that we have been disobedient, we automatically feel a sense of guilt which causes us to rebel. Think about it. It's true. It's a weird thing we do. It is exactly what the nation of Israel did. As soon as God said, "Thou shalt not..." the people rebelled. It's been that way since the moment Adam and Eve were presented with free choice.

We seem to think that obedience is all about doing something we *must* do. But when we begin to understand the magnitude of God's love for us, obedience becomes something we *want* to do.

Obedience to God is vastly different to the obedience we are accustomed to in our human understanding of the term. We automatically feel that we have to give something up to be obedient. We feel that we might miss out on something better. We have FOMO. (Fear of Missing Out). Satan knew exactly how to trap Adam and Eve with their free will. He knew how to use the gift that God had given them to his advantage.

Then the serpent said to the woman, "You will not surely die. For God knows that in the day you eat of [the fruit of the tree] your eyes will be opened, and you will be like God, knowing good and evil." - Genesis 3:4-5

Satan fueled Adam and Eve's free choice with options that could ultimately end in their disconnecting from the One who had given them life. Satan twisted what had been spoken to make them believe that God was withholding something from them which Satan had no right to do. God has given us every right to evaluate the options before us. He simply desires us to be motivated by His love and truth in making those decisions. Unlike Satan, God *gets* us because He *made* us.

We have a built in monitor that checks up on our decision making effectiveness. We have a hunger to, at the very least, try to get our next decision right. This comes from our built in desire to improve our lot in life. To get fitter, to be slimmer or to earn more. But are our motives right?

We always want the result of our decisions to bring us the highest possible gain. This is where we need to change our perspective of obedience. When we generally make decisions, our thoughts are on the outcome. The best possible results in the immediate make us believe that we have made a good decision. We have been so side swiped by the consequences of what Satan set in motion that we have begun to share Adam and Eve's FOMO. We are led to believe that there must be something better and that making God honoring decisions could leave us worse off. For example, Scripture asks us to love our enemies and bless them. We may think in the moment that loving our enemies is just not natural. We couldn't possibly be wired to do something as crazy as blessing those who curse us. Deep down, however, we know that it's the right thing to do. That's because we were wired by a God of love. We begin to make decisions based not on a selfish outcome but rather on a God honoring motivation.

When we are selfishly obedient, we have made the wrong decision. When we make decisions to ensure that God is honored, then that is the optimal decision. God honoring, free will decisions result when we begin to understand that His love *is* the very best for us. We are not given His love by being obedient, we are obedient because of His love.

It is because of His love that we exist. It is because of His love that we can do all things. It is because of His love that we want to, in our free will, choose to love Him back. We give Him free will obedience *because* of His love.

CHAPTER THREE
"I LOVE IT WHEN A PLAN COMES TOGETHER"

See, I have set before you today life and good, death and evil, in that I command you today to love the Lord your God, to walk in His ways, and to keep His commandments, His statutes, and His judgments, that you may live and multiply; and the Lord your God will bless you in the land which you go to possess. - Deuteronomy 30:15-16

In South Africa there is an old Afrikaans saying: " 'n Boer maak 'n plan!" Translated it means that a farmer always makes a plan. It's like having the attitude of the notorious McGuyver, and always being able to create something out of nothing. Colonel John "Hannibal" Smith of the A-Team loved it when his "plan came together," or perhaps it's more like Bob the Builder. "Can we fix it? Yes we can."

I am not just referring to these TV programs or Afrikaans proverb to reveal my age, but also to demonstrate that we all too often try to fix what is broken, *on our own*. We try to fix our lives in interesting ways. We try to do things using our own strength. We are constantly attempting to fill in the spiritual hole that is in each of us. We feel an emptiness that needs filling for us to be complete. We so badly want our lives to have meaning and purpose that we envision a plan of our own creation. Often we come up with unwise belief systems through which we try to reason a life plan into being, or, if you were like me, partied to fill that hole. We all seek the ideal: a life of fulfillment.

We want the blessings. We want to feel whole and complete. We don't want to feel that life is defeating us and our life experiences are breaking us. So, we think that a good deed here or there is going to quench our thirst for fulfillment. Christ defined this for the Samaritan women at the well. She had made some pretty shocking decisions and some pretty crazy plans to fix her situation. But Jesus recognized in her a thirst to get it right and improve her lot in life.

Jesus replied, "Anyone who drinks this water will soon become thirsty again. But those who drink the water I give will never be thirsty again. It becomes a fresh, bubbling spring within them, giving them eternal life." – John 4:13-14

She desired to unlock true and sustainable blessings. She was intrigued by the possibilities of having long lasting meaning, purpose and Godly inspiration. She wanted the living water that Jesus spoke of as opposed to drawing literal water from the well.

"Please, sir," the woman said, "give me this water! Then I'll never be thirsty again, and I won't have to come here to get water." – John 4:15

With her history, the women did not feel that she was worthy. She tried to make excuses when Jesus offered her the opportunity. She even deflected the conversation with first academic questions…

"But sir, you don't have a rope or a bucket," she said, "and this well is very deep. Where would you get this living water? And besides, do you think you're greater than our ancestor Jacob, who gave us this well? How can you offer better water than he and his sons and his animals enjoyed?" – John 4:11-12

and then a theological question.

> *"Sir," the woman said, "you must be a prophet. So tell me, why is it that you Jews insist that Jerusalem is the only place of worship, while we Samaritans claim it is here at Mount Gerizim, where our ancestors worshiped?" - John 4:19*

She could not perceive the incredible God on the other end of the offer. She wrestled with wrong and right in her life and she had tried to solve her own issues in her own way, but her plan wasn't working for her. She still had that gnawing spiritual hole that needed to be filled in a divine way rather than in the way she chose to fill it.

Just like that Samaritan women, our search for palatable answers to unlocking the blessings of God in our lives by adding our own solutions, deeds and thoughts to the process has caused us to paint a picture of God that reduces Him to a mere shadow of His true magnificence.

Some of us have begun to see God rather like an accountant and our relationship with Him as a business transaction. In exchange for our deposit of an obedient action, right decision or correct religious activity, we anticipate His reward with interest.

Others feel that asking the right question or studying the right theology will put back that true sense of deep inspiration. Just like the Pharisees, our journey becomes religious and we stick to the liturgy of belief rather than claim new ground and make inspired Godly choices through personal revelation. Many churches have become a collection of people convinced that they are inspired. They talk and act like they are inspired. Some television evangelists even sweat like they are inspired. Generally, however, many Christians live powerless lives of emptiness and hurt because they trust God for a moment and expect a lifetime of blessings.

…having a form of godliness but denying its power.
– 2 Timothy 3:5a

Perhaps another perspective some have is that God does not really exist or that His existence makes no logical sense. We would sit and quibble over ridiculous ideas like evolution or debate His very existence, rather than change our thought process and begin arriving at meaningful conclusions based on the Word. We will never change who God is, but we can change who we become by changing how we think about God.

Do not conform any longer to the pattern of this

world, but be transformed by the renewing of your mind. Then you will be able to test and approve what God's will is—his good, pleasing and perfect will. - Romans 12:2

Some people I have met along the way believe that they could never be good enough to be loved so much by God. Rather than enjoy His love; they believe that God wouldn't stoop low enough to actively participate in their meaningless, unimportant lives. They have never encountered a true and personal relationship with Him. They doubt that they could ever be good enough to be part of His plan and are incapable of recognizing and understanding that God loves them unconditionally. They believe that they would have to get their lives completely in order before God would unlock any blessings He might have for them.

Still others know God exists but would rather reason things through for themselves and make life decisions with no regard for God's principles. They pray just to let God know of their plans and decisions. They would rather excuse core principles in the Bible in favor of their own moral code. They feel that God knew what he was doing when He breathed the galaxy into being or parted the Red Sea, but He could not possibly understand the complexities of their situation.

When people question God's presence in their lives, it is probably because they have felt disappointed by Him, by the church, as they know it, by the Bible or by any combination thereof. Whatever place they find themselves, they need to consider two things. First, what decisions have *they* made and what plans have *they* developed to arrive where they are. Second, they must take a good hard look at their true motives for making those plans. If they cannot link their decisions to God's Divine plan and are not motivated by a love for Him, they have created for themselves an ongoing struggle which precludes any long term sustainable benefits or blessings. In fact, those decisions can be responsible for unnecessary hurt and pain.

What it boils down to is simply taking a chance and trusting God by making decisions with no other motive other than to give honor to Him. We call it blind faith with a hint of free will.

But, in the simplicity of our understanding of God, we have taught ourselves that obedience to God's law always leads to blessings. This destructive belief alienates people from God rather than ensuring a solid and meaningful communion with Him. Individuals who feel that they are obedient to the letter of the law are seldom able to understand why bad things happen to them. When God does not immediately match their good deed with a good blessing, they often doubt His very existence and turn away from Him confused and hurt.

The Scribes and the Pharisees of Jesus' time, truly believed that they were the epitome of obedience and yet despite being in a place of a supposed blessing, Jesus called them "white washed graves" and "offspring of vipers." They had adhered to the letter of the law and had even created more of their own laws to show God how obedient they were. Their choices were the furthest thing from Gods optimal way.

This calls into question our understanding that obedience alone brings about automatic blessing. When driving, I can adhere to the letter of the traffic code, but that does not necessarily mean I will never be involved in a motor vehicle accident. By simply adhering to a few biblical laws we are not guaranteed to walk through this life without difficulty and calamity. Does obedience mean that if we read our Bible and live a good life that we are truly stepping into the blessings of God?

It does in part, but there is an aspect of the journey that we have conveniently ignored. It is in fact the most important element, and it is revealed in the way that Satan approached Adam and Eve.

Satan did not try to show that God would refuse to bless Adam and Eve if they were disobedient. Even he knew that he could not disprove a divine principle. Instead, he simply removed their motivation for choosing God's optimal way. He planted a seed that would cause Eve to question what she knew to be true of God. The Godly way was all she knew and up until then it was the perfect choice prompted by trust in her loving God. That was what motivated everything in her life. She knew He had her best interests at heart. It was that motivation alone that brought about her sense of perfect fulfillment. Satan needed only to cause her to doubt whether or not God had her best interests at heart. Satan knew that he could get her to question why she was obedient to God, if he could convince her that God was withholding something from her. Satan distorted her sense of clarity and vision. He tempted her where he knew he would cause the most mayhem. He simply caused her to question the trust she had in her Heavenly Father.

Now the serpent was more cunning than any beast of the field which the LORD God had made. And he said to the woman, "Has God indeed said, 'You shall not eat of every tree of the garden'?"

And the woman said to the serpent, "We may eat the fruit of the trees of the garden; but of the fruit of the tree which is in the midst of the garden, God has said, **'You shall not eat it, nor shall you touch it, lest you die.'"** *Then the serpent said to the woman, "You will not surely die. For God knows that in the day you eat of it your eyes will be opened, and you will be like God, knowing good and evil."- Genesis 3:4-5 (Emphasis mine)*

Without trust, obedience instantly falters. A lie breaks the bond of trust and because Satan knew that broken trust in God would break mankind's obedience, he sowed lies into the minds of Adam and Eve just as he sows lies into our minds today to break our trust, obedience and our close personal relationships with God.

Before that fateful day, there was no doubt in Eve's mind that she trusted God. As a result, she was completely motivated to do what God asked her to do. She trusted implicitly that what God asked of her was always in her best interest. She had no reason to think that God would ever cause her harm or withhold something from her (FOMO). Satan, however, caused her to question the very essence of her reason to be obedient. Today, we have allowed that doubt to grow to such an extent that, like Eve, it completely overshadows our trust in and resultant obedience to God. It was not God who was tricked into not trusting us. He has a plan for every outcome.

The shame of making the wrong decision, the embarrassment of realizing their own frailty washed over Adam and Eve causing them to hide from God. Even in their fallen state, God still desired a relationship with them, but they could not get past the guilt of having mistrusted their Creator and Heavenly Father.

Once the guilt was a distant memory for Adam and Eve, the consequences of their behavior began to turn what was once a flawless love for God into anger toward Him. We all know that there's a very "thin line between love and hate" from the 70's song title (I was born in the 70's). Satan's lie began to take Adam and Eve's feelings of shame and embarrassment and turn them into deep feelings of insecurity, guilt, hurt, hate, anger, bitterness and selfishness in an effort to maintain the chasm between them and God. When we look at all that is God—His infinite love and His amazing desire for us to thrive and be blessed—none of these Satanic attributes fit.

But the fruit of the Spirit is love, joy, peace, long suffering, kindness, goodness, faithfulness, gentleness, self-control. Against such there is no law. - Galatians 5:22-23

When I look at the list of the fruit of the Spirit, I often find myself wondering why anyone would try to make their own plan when the results are devoid of any of this kind of fruit. That same chapter in the Bible also describes the results of Satan's lie and the consequences of our plans to artificially fill the relationship that we were designed to have with God.

Now the works of the flesh are evident, which are: adultery, fornication, uncleanness, lewdness, idolatry, sorcery, hatred, contentions, jealousies, outbursts of wrath, selfish ambitions, dissensions, heresies, envy, murders, drunkenness, revelries, and the like; of which I tell you beforehand, just as I also told you in time past, that those who practice such things will not inherit the kingdom of God. - Galatians 5:19-21

Perhaps you have been making a plan, coming up with your own answers and doing things your way. How is it working out for you? Which of these scriptures in Galatians better describes the fruit of your decision making, the fruit of the Spirit or the fruit of the flesh?

We may never have all the answers, but God does through scripture. Does hell exist? Is there really a place called heaven? Where do we go when we die? I am generally a good person; why do I need to go to church? My money is my money; why should I give it away? Apes are definitely part of my family tree!

There are only two options set before us, to blindly trust a God who has never wronged us, or try and figure it out on our own and reap what we sow. In my life and in my experience, trying to figure it out on my own landed me in a police holding cell in Hilbrow Johannesburg, South Africa. In that cell all those years ago, God asked me some life changing questions: "How's it going with doing it your way, Craig? Are you ready to do it my way now?"

> *See, I have set before you today life and good, death and evil, in that I command you today to love the Lord your God, to walk in His ways, and to keep His commandments, His statutes, and His judgments, that you may live and multiply; and the Lord your God will bless you in the land which you go to possess. - Deuteronomy 30:15-16*

In scripture, when God asks us to do something, it is never without a reason. He always asks us to do what is in our best interest. When God tells us *not* to do something, it is never without a reason either. It is to protect us from harm. All too often, as we saw with Eve in the garden of Eden, we have an automatic reaction that causes us to question whether He truly has our best interests at heart.

We still have the choice. He gives us the principles by which we should be making decisions. He has wired them into us. Instead of interacting with us like He did with Adam and Eve, He has laid those principles out in the form of an instruction manual, the Bible, and uses scripture to remind us of what He has written on the tablet of our hearts. All He wants from us is to freely choose His way because we completely trust that His "thou shalts" and "thou shalt nots" are in our best interests.

CHAPTER FOUR
GRAVITY RULES

"Order my steps in Your word; and let not any iniquity have dominion over me." - Psalm 119: 133

I had a brilliant math teacher in high school. According to school rumor, he was a genius. It was thought that on rare occasions he could be heard uttering mathematical equations under his breath in fluent Latin. He even had that typical crazy professor look about him. I knew how brilliant he was because although we read from the same textbooks, he understood what he was reading. As you have probably gathered by now, academic challenges were placed in my life to keep me humble.

Anyway, this math teacher would go on and on about the unchangeable principles of the universe. He would not let us leave class without reminding us that no matter what the problem, whether we were working on geometrical or algebraic problems, there were indisputable laws that governed our calculations.

I thought that the indisputable law of my mathematics bordered more on the illogical laws of chaos than the neat order of a mathematical solution.

Since those days in a classroom in Wynberg, Cape Town, South Africa, not much has changed. Today my mathematics teacher is my Heavenly Father and His genius is not rumored. He is desperate for me to understand that spiritual chaos is ordered through indisputable divine principles that He has wired into my DNA.

No matter what gifting, ability, situation or problem we may have, no matter how we have previously tried to resolve issues and burdens, no matter how confused or lost we feel, no matter how unworthy or useless we may feel about ourselves, there are some basic divine principles that will help us choose the optimal solution to any given situation.

When we become sold out to these principles, our trust becomes evident. If needs be, we should be willing to simply and blindly accept these principles based completely on the deep sense of knowing of God's love for us. We don't need more than that. We don't need another reason, academic explanation or personal benefit to trust His principles. The sole motivator should be His love for us. His love is the basis of His divine principles, and it should also be the sole motivator for us to apply those principles to our lives.

John 14:15 puts it simply when it says, "If you love me, you will obey what I command."

Once we begin to be obedient to God simply based on the fact that we trust in Him and in His love for us, we are doing way more than just doing what He tells us to do. We are getting to know Him, we are growing in our love for Him, and we are building a personal, intimate relationship with Him. If that's what we seek, then attention to the divine principles that have been placed in us is a must, not an option. We can't only want to obey because the principles seem beneficial in the now. We can't have an intimate relationship with God and then ignore His words and principles. Being obedient to God is not the same as sticking to the speed limit because we may be fined if we disobey. Obedience to

God is living God's Word and His principles because we want to and not because we have to and will be punished if we do not. We must simply enjoy pleasing Him by loving Him and trusting in Him unconditionally.

God's principles have been spoken and instituted by God Himself. He has put them in place to make sure that we who love Him will never lose ourselves in the chaos of this life. He does this because He is excited about spending eternity with us, and He does not want this life to rob us of the joy that awaits us with Him in His Kingdom.

God has not put these principles in place to limit us. He places no limits on our ability to decide things for ourselves. He wants us to make up our own minds. He has designed us to voluntarily choose Him because it gives Him great joy and because He wants to know us. He wants us to experience the fullness of this beautiful life that He has created for us. He wants us to come to certain realizations about our lives by being able to be guided and taught through His core principles.

Pearl S. Buck said: *"Order is the shape upon which beauty depends."* Our God has shaped order from our disheveled lives, making it beautiful by placing divine principles in place that not even He would contravene.

These principles are as real and as evident as laws of nature. They have as much spiritual impact on humankind as natural laws, such as the law of gravity, have on nature.

For thousands of years, we have been taught about God. We have been taught about the Old Testament vengeance and wrath, and we have been taught about the New Testament grace and love. Little is done, however, to teach the application of divine principles from scripture. We can revolutionize the way we live life if we truly trust and believe these divine principles and the love upon which they are based.

I never got the big picture of my God until I started studying and understanding the principles that He put in place for my benefit. I never completely saw the full face of my Heavenly Father until I began seeing Him through the divine principles that He instituted to make sure that I could live a life that would impact humanity for the Kingdom.

From the beginning, we have been given a choice as to whether or not to live by these divine principles. We have an unrestricted right to say "YES!" to the principles of God. We don't have to be mathematical geniuses to look around and see that there is nothing else to choose from that will bring the kind of life that God has in mind for us.

Allowing Him to order our steps will ensure that the discouraging effects of worldly principles will no longer have power over us. Psalm 119:133, says, *"Order my steps in Your word; and let not any iniquity have dominion over me."* In other words, take the stand for God's principles in our lives and nothing of this world will have the power to conquer us.

King David writes of his Heavenly Father:

"Every word you give me is a miracle word – how can I help but obey? Break open your words; let the light shine out, let ordinary people see the meaning. Mouth open and panting, I wanted your commands more than anything. Turn my way; look kindly on me, as you always do to those who personally love you. Steady my steps with your Word of promise so nothing malign gets the better of me. Rescue me from the grip of bad men and women so I can live life your way. Smile on me, teach me the right way to live. I cry rivers of tears because nobody's living by your book!" - *Psalm 119:126-136 (The Message Bible)*

We are to ask God to "steady our steps," so that nothing unrighteous will rule or be given power over us. The order or framing of our steps by Gods principles are what will shape our lives, give us meaning and direction and keep us from harm.

Belief in the principles He has put in place must become as real as the physical laws we can see or experience.

For example, if I were to drop a glass, I know that it would fall to the floor. There is that split second when I try to catch it or attempt to prevent it from hitting the ground. However, I know that gravity will not fail. I may try to prevent the results of gravity, but I know that I cannot escape its effect. The glass will shatter when it hits the floor.

The same is true of every one of Gods divine principles. Be it gravity or blessings, motion or promises, energy or grace, the principles of God have been ordered and set in place and they are irrefutable. Whether physical or divine they all originate from God and have the same unfailing attributes.

Our challenge in this life is to grow to completely trust in God's divine principles and to trust them in our lives as much as we trust in the physical ones.

At first it may be as simple as learning a divine principle like the one found in Luke 6:31 where we are told to *"do to others as you would have them do to you."*

As we grow, however, we will need to apply that principle to other matters. Perhaps it would have us applying that principle to a business contract, church work or a family issue. The depth of our trust in Godly principles can be measured directly by how readily we are willing to apply them throughout all of our life situations.

To illustrate, if we were only to take the theory of gravity to mean that when something is dropped it will fall, we will never apply the principles of gravity to other things such as tides and waves. Our oceans are impacted by those same gravitational principles that shattered a glass, but the effect is vastly different when we holiday at the beach. The same is true of the divine principles of God. The principles remain true, but the applications and effects are endless.

Trust is evidenced by how we apply God's principles and whether or not we passionately live our lives according to them. It would mean not just knowing God's principles but growing in the understanding that they originate from His infinite love and grace and allow ourselves to continue growing as we use them passionately in our daily lives. This is the true beginning of understanding. When we grasp these truths, and trust God to help us apply them, God's heart rejoices as He watches us discover His optimal plan to a blessed life.

Trust is a direct result of our full revelation of God's love and grace in our lives. Love and grace are the reason that God inspired His principles to be written in the bible and wired into us. They are also the reason why God wants us to obey them. He wants us to love Him enough and to trust Him enough to be obedient to Him. He wants us to trust Him simply because we love Him and not because of our desire to be blessed. He does not want us to believe that He blesses us based on our actions (obedience). He blesses us based on what motivates us to adhere to His principles. He blesses us solely and simply because He loves us and because we demonstrate our love for Him by being obedient to his principles.

Without grasping the depth of that love, we may superficially appear to trust God's principles because they work well in our lives or look good on the mantel piece of people's perceptions of us. This is man-made love motivated only by self-fulfillment and does not inspire a sense of awe in our Heavenly Father. Limiting the effects of God's principles by making unintentional changes to them or deliberately shaping them to benefit our lives is not what God had in mind for us when He spoke them into being. Losing ourselves in them is what will maximize our trust and as a result maximize our obedience; maximized obedience then results in maximized blessings. So we learn, just like the scribes and Pharisees that we can't just leap frog into obedience just to obtain blessings. We must start at the beginning and love our God with a love which is based on and evidenced primarily by one dramatic and historical event—the arrival of Jesus Christ.

Now that we better understand the concepts of love, trust, and obedience, and God's plan for our lives, let's consider these primary principles that unlock a life of blessing. Theologians and inspirational authors may well be able to dispute my choice of principles to discuss here, but it is these key principles that I have applied and accepted into my life. I wasn't always sold out to the principles of God. I was often hurt and caused much hurt to others by living life based on my own principles. The principles of God, however, have changed my marriage, have taught me how to be a Godly father and to love my children and have allowed God's vision and direction to explode into my life.

The promises of God will come to pass and will endure. God is always truthful. He is the maker of the universe. He is my God and there is no other. My Heavenly Father loved me for no benefit, and He simply asks me to love Him in return.

CHAPTER FIVE
MIRROR MIRROR

So God created man in His own image; in the image of God He created him; Male and female He created them.

- Genesis 1:27

We have already established that I am no Pythagoras (For those of you who don't know, he was one of the greatest mathematicians that ever lived.) nor am I remotely as talented as Johan Borman (a renowned South African impressionist artist). I wish I could draw and sketch. One thing that I have always wanted to be able to do is draw a horse. In elementary school I had to use a magazine cut out image of a horse instead of draw one of my own, while a girl in my class, Natalie, reached for her Crayola crayons and drew a horse that looked as though it could gallop right off the page. She was very good to say the least. I really thought that her secret was that she had at her disposal a big box of Crayola crayons.

She could reach for colors such as "Tumbleweed", "Sunset Orange" and my personal favorite "Cobalt Blue."

I tried everything, including convincing my parents to buy me a big box of crayons just like Natalie's—my horse artist nemesis. I decided I would check a book out of the local library that used basic shapes to guide my drawing. It taught how to draw almost anything including horses, but my horse always looked like a duck with the head of a T-Rex or a T-Rex with the head of a duck. I never quite decided which.

God has never had a problem with creativity. When I thought of Genesis 2:27 which told me that I was made in God's image, and I compared my picture of God with the picture of my life, I felt like a duck with the head of a T-Rex.

If He made me in His image, surely there should be at least some of His features in me. Yet as I looked through the list of the highs and lows of my life, I could not find the kind of love that came anywhere near to the infinite love that God has for me. I did not have any of the strength that reflected His power. I certainly made decisions that I have no doubt insulted His wisdom. I know that to Him, my selfishness looked like dirty laundry alongside His judicial robes.

When it came to wrapping my mind around the fact that God loves me, I just could not accept that I was good enough to be loved by Him, let alone be made in His image.

It was more than just the fact that I did not have a very good earthly father figure as a comparison, or that I had been dragged through a heavy-handed religious upbringing. I just did not feel like I was anything like Him. I even had a scripture to support my feelings:

But we are all like an unclean thing, And all our righteousnesses are like filthy rags; We all fade as a leaf, And our iniquities, like the wind, Have taken us away. - Isaiah 64:6

I read the account of us being made in Gods image in Genesis again and again, until one day the answer came to me. God made me in His image *before* the deceptions of Satan were woven into the human psyche. Anything then that convinced me that I was not made in His image was based on deception. The same deception that swayed Adam and Eve. The truth was that because of my belief in His divine gift of Jesus Christ, God looked upon me just as He looked upon Adam and Eve on the

6th day of creation: complete, whole, sin free and "very good." When I allowed sin and deception to creep into my life, it was not God's image of me that changed, it was the same guilt and shame that Adam and Eve felt when they believed the deception that gave them cause to hide from God.

"Imago Dei" is the Hebrew root of the Latin phrase for "image of God," and it more accurately means image, shadow or likeness of God. Humans are a snapshot or facsimile of God. It does not by any stretch of the imagination mean that we *are* God. It does not mean, as some new thinking would have us believe, that God exists as a collective from the thoughts and beliefs of all humans. It means that we are godlike which I will discuss further as we go on.

I doubt that there is a single human who doesn't want the answer to why they feel a gap between who they want to be (in God's image) and who they punish themselves for being (as a result of Satan's deception). As humans, we invent things to fill that gap, and when we don't feel fulfilled, we fabricate our own solutions which leads us even further away from the true fulfillment God has for us. Instead of being godlike, we set ourselves up to be our own gods. We place ourselves in charge and make our own decisions. We decide that we don't need a Jesus or a god or even an eternal future—"who knows about that for sure?" we ask. We fabricate belief structures that hide our inadequacies and which feed into our human selfishness—like Adam and Eve.

If we are a picture or a snapshot of God, to truly be able to discover who we are and what we should believe we need to look at the subject of the picture–God himself. Then if we find that the attributes of God match some of the more fulfilling elements that we find ourselves searching for, we will have a source that we can study to find answers for life's most perplexing questions. The source of which I speak, is the God of the Bible, the God who provided Jesus Christ and the God that holds the entire universe together. He is the expert when it comes to who we are—after all He wired us in His image.

One of the attributes we can look at in an effort to understand how we are made in God's image is the hope we have once we find Jesus. Human beings have an instinctive ability to hope and believe for better things. We dream and imagine and cast vision. Businesses are founded on vision statements, dreams are written in journals and we turn our fantasies into bucket lists. Why do we do this? Because humans hope to accomplish the things they dream of. We may never see some of the things we hope for, but we hope for them nonetheless. The Bible describes it like this:

> *Now **faith** is the substance of things **hoped** for, the evidence of things not seen. - Hebrews 11:1 (emphasis mine)*

No other creature in the universe does this. No fossil record can provide evidence from where this desire evolved. Subhuman animals cannot have faith or hope, because no other creature besides man was made in the image and likeness of God. God Himself is the source of faith and hope. It stands to reason then that God who has offered hope to humankind, has hope and faith Himself. God is the source of our faith and the reason we hope for better things. God and His faithfulness and the hope He offers are the root causes of us searching for something more, something better: to live happily ever after as it were. We have that longing because God has that longing for us as well. Our hope to be loved and to love, our hope for happiness and our hope for better things did not start with us. It started with God and is mirrored in us. We are a copy of God who hopes that we love Him as much as He loves us and who hopes that we will discover faith in Him, a faith that surmounts the deceptions that rob us of the peace He provides for us. We can have His hope and faith even though we cannot see or touch Him.

Another attribute that existed in me that I struggled to make sense of was my creativity. Now I may not be able to draw a horse, but one thing I know is that somehow, I have the ability to be creative. I have never been able to understand how or where my creativity came from until, there it was in the very first verse in the Bible.

*In the beginning God **created** the heavens and the earth" - Genesis 1:1*

God is creative. Therefore, it stands to reason that if man is made in His image, we stand out from the rest of the universe in our ability to create. And we do. Poets, writers, artists, architects, engineers, inventors and almost every human being has an innate ability to mirror their maker and creator. No scientific reasoning or fossil record will validate us any more simply than the Biblical truth that we are a copy of the Creator and have, therefore, inherited His creative nature.

Let's look at some more of God's attributes that exist

within us as humans that have no other possible explanation for their existence other than being mirrored features of the Most High God.

For example, humans have a deep desire to understand things spiritual. God is spirit.

God is Spirit, and those who worship Him must worship in spirit and truth. -John 4:24

The Bible verifies our mirrored spiritual image of God.

*Now may the God of peace Himself sanctify you completely; and may your whole **spirit**, soul, and body be preserved blameless at the coming of our Lord Jesus Christ. - 1 Thessalonians 5:23 (emphasis mine)*

We have an intelligence that far surpasses other living creatures. Where does this intelligence come from? God is intelligence.

*In the beginning was the **Word** and the **Word** was with God, and the **Word** was God. - John 1:1 (emphasis mine)*

Besides referencing Jesus Christ, Word in this verse comes from the Greek word "logos," which means amongst other things, reason or logic. The universe that Jesus was part of creating, screams out organization, logic and order and provides evidence that it could only be the result of a source of intelligence. The only source of intelligence—God Himself.

The heavens declare the glory of God; And the firmament shows His handiwork. - Psalm 19:1

The word logos refers to God and, therefore, likewise to us, as having not just intellect alone, but also having an ability to *process* and to create logic and order through thought and reason.

John Donne wrote a poem he entitled, "No Man is an Island." It simply states the principle that man has a deep desire to live relationally. It is far deeper than just an animalistic instinct to find a mate or move with the pack. We gain deep emotional fulfillment from being relational. God is relational too. In fact, He describes His relational attributes before He created man.

*Then God said, "Let **Us** make man in **Our** image, according to **Our** likeness; - Genesis 1:26a (emphasis mine)*

God is clear in Genesis that He was not operating alone. He referred to there being an *us*. Once he created Adam in His own image, God understood that because He was relational that Adam would also have the desire to be relational.

And the Lord God said, "It is not good that man should be alone; I will make him a helper comparable to him. - Genesis 2:18

God then created Eve for Adam because "it is not good for man to be alone." This was done out of love and a knowledge that the same relational attribute that existed in God would now exist and be wired into mankind.

And so it continues. Every aspect of our makeup for which we struggle to find reasons or sources, can be simply explained in the principle that we were made in the image of our Creator. We have a built-in desire for certain things because we were made with similar desires to God. It is up to us to manage those desires and allow them to be used to honor and glorify God rather than to allow them to be used and consumed by Satan's deceptions.

Jesus understood this principle. He walked so perfectly in the image of God that when one of His own asked Jesus to show him the Father, Jesus responded by asking Phillip a question.

Jesus said to him, "Have I been with you so long, and yet you have not known Me, Philip? He who has seen Me has seen the Father; so how can you say, 'Show us the Father'? - John 14:9

In other words, how can we question that God exists? Just look at all the wonderful, unexplainable qualities and attributes in us and these alone are proof that God exists. We are made in His image. It's by His choice that we have Him within us.

If you ever get to meet my youngest son Kyle, this concept is easily demonstrated. Kyle has often been called "mini-Smee." There is no denying that he is my son. He looks like me and has specific attributes that are clearly from his dad. Would it make sense for him to deny my existence or say that he comes from his pet cat? In many ways, despite being his own person with free will, he mirrors me.

The principle of being made in God's image gives us an identity and an awesome sense of belonging when we are able to grasp it. When we know where we come from, we can know where we are going. Knowing that we have the attributes of our heavenly Father, means that we come from Him. It also means that what God says about us is true and that we are going to be with Him. He alone is our source and our eternal destination. Consider His spirit, creativity, intellect, logic, faith and hope.

These attributes should make sense to us because they are part of who we are.

CHAPTER SIX
KNOW, NOW DO

For I also am a man under authority, having soldiers under me. And I say to this one, 'Go,' and he goes; and to another, 'Come,' and he comes; and to my servant, 'Do this,' and he does it." - Matthew 8:9

As you may have already deduced, I was born in South Africa. While there, I worked at Cape Town Fire and Rescue Services for a while.

It always amazed me to see how some of the men I was privileged to work with changed in their behavior and personality as they rose through the ranks. When one of them would receive a promotion to the rank of officer, he was required to turn in part of his uniform at the fire station's store in exchange for the uniform required for his new rank.

Officers were required to wear white shirts and not light blue ones like the general firemen. It was a special day when they wore their white shirt for the first time. It was interesting to watch these new officers appear at role call in their new uniforms. Some of them fit the role from day one, while others needed some time to adapt to their new role. The point is that their behavior changed when they received their rank and its corresponding uniform. It was easy to accept that their rank had changed, but the authority associated with that rank took some getting used to.

I recently preached a message series that was based on the statement, *"When you know who you are, you will know what to do."* When we understand who we are from God's perspective it changes how we behave. When we take on the rank and authority that God purposed for us, it should change the way we act. As Christians, we can easily become lost in this world if we lose touch with who we are. When God created us in His image, He made humankind to be in authority, to take charge and to shape a whole new world. God planned for us to be officers and stewards of this world. We were made in His image and that image comes complete with all the rank and authority of the Most High God.

We're not meant to usurp that authority by barking orders at others or demanding respect. It's a God given authority that empowers us to take charge over our lives and our enemy, Satan, who tries to steal and destroy our life giving relationship with God.

We cannot have this authority unless we accept that we are under the authority of the one who gave it. This authority gives us the right to govern our own lives in a purposeful manner. When we commit to God and Jesus Christ, we step into that authority which allows us to leave behind our old life and self, a self that had been accustomed to living by the seat of our pants, as it were.

Senior Pastor Craig Groeschel of Life Church in Oklahoma writes in his book Chazown that *"many people will get somewhere, but few get somewhere on purpose."* When we take up our God given authority and begin to seriously live the vision that God has for us, we begin to make decisions based upon Him and not upon what the world prescribes. That is when we discover that our individual rhythm in life will be one which allows us to breathe and gives us the freedom to make Godly decisions and not spur-of-the-moment emotionally charged ones.

When we step away from that purpose driven authority, we lose our way and tend to forget who we are in Christ. At that point we begin to flounder through life with no sense of purpose or direction, forgetting our authority and certainly have little joy and peace. Adam and Eve are the perfect example of this breakdown.

When this happens, where has our sense of remembering who we are, our purpose and God given authority gone? To understand our authority, we need to backtrack to when we, as humans, received our Godly authority, how we lost it and finally how we regained it.

So God created man in His own image; in the image of God He created him; male and female He created them. Then God blessed them, and God said to them, "Be fruitful and multiply; fill the earth and subdue it; have dominion over the fish of the sea, over the birds of the air, and over every living thing that moves on the earth." - Genesis 1:27-28

When God created man, He designed a human DNA template that contained some fundamental principles wired into it. The first, we have already discussed, in that you were made in His image. According to Genesis there is more. "Then God blessed them." How did He bless them? What did He add to His image that would cause blessing? He blessed them by giving them a purpose and authority. The purpose in Adam and Eve's situation was to "be fruitful and multiply, fill the earth and subdue it." To that purpose, He then added authority or dominion over the things of this earth. He gave them a job description and a "white shirt" to get the job done.

If we truly want to live a life full of blessing, all day every day blessing, and not be constantly begging God for one bail out miracle after another, we must first appreciate what it means to be made in His image, then we can grasp our purpose. Finally, we can step into the authority we have been given.

Sadly, it was not enough for Adam and Eve to be made in God's image, to have a purpose and to walk in their God given authority. They decided to relinquish their right to Satan, who had been given no authority on earth, to direct themselves. Man had been given that dominion by God. The only way Satan could gain authority was for man to surrender it to him. Once God had given authority to man, it became his to decide— free will—what he would do with it. Adam and Eve changed the course of world history by giving control to Satan. They did not lose their identity as human beings, however, they still had a job to do and a purpose to fulfill; they had given up their authority by choice. They no longer had the ability to take charge over their surroundings which would now take charge over them. Satan could plague them, tempt them, entice them, they became his toys to manipulate as he saw fit. Had they lived in our time, Satan could have used advertising or political rhetoric to control their feelings and emotions. They would have been controlled by their illnesses and ailments and completely tied to "an endless, self-defeating, and pointless pursuit we call the 'rat race'." (Wikipedia) They chose not to honor God but rather allow their senses of guilt and shame to direct their behavior. They believed that they were failures and allowed that sense of failure to control them.

Speaking negatively and being governed by what other people think of us, or what we think of ourselves are the results of allowing each of our situations to dictate to us who we are and how we feel. Accepting the deception of no self-worth or feelings of uselessness are ways we give over our authority. The world and Satan will never stop bombarding us with messages that are trying to "rob, steal and destroy" our purpose (John 10:10). Giving up our authority only happens, however, when we start believing the deceptions.

Honor God and we regain our authority. Listen to the deceptions of Satan, and we lose it.

What did God do to make sure there was a certain way for us to regain the authority that Adam and Eve lost on our behalf?

He sent Jesus Christ and took Him through the same process that Adam had gone through. God wasn't trying to punish Jesus but rather, in part, to ensure that we had an earthly example of how to maintain our authority. Jesus gave up His divine placement to take back the earthly authority that Adam and Eve had lost for humanity. The only way he was able to do that was to come to earth as a man, because that authority was originally given by God to man on earth.

In the beginning was the Word, and the Word was with God, and the Word was God. He was in the beginning with God. All things were made through Him, and without Him nothing was made that was made. In Him was life, and the life was the light of men. And the light shines in the darkness, and the darkness did not comprehend it. - John 1:1-5

And the Word became flesh and dwelt among us, and we beheld His glory, the glory as of the only begotten of the Father, full of grace and truth. - John 1:14

At Jesus' baptism, He received His authority in exactly the same way as Adam did. Adam was made in God's image. He knew who he was because he knew where he had come from. Being made by God and in God's image gave him an understanding of his true identity. At Jesus' baptism God did the same for Jesus.

While he was still speaking, behold, a bright cloud overshadowed them; and suddenly a voice came out of the cloud, saying, **"This is My beloved Son, in whom I am well pleased.** *Hear Him!" - Matthew 17:5 (emphasis mine)*

God gave Adam an identity and was pleased (Genesis 1:31). God gave Jesus, an identity and was pleased (Matthew 17:5). God established Jesus on earth as a man to demonstrate to us how to take back our identity, authority and purpose. *When we know who we are we will know what to do.* When we walk in that authority, identity and purpose, God is pleased.

As Jesus went into the desert after his baptism and was tempted by Satan, Jesus clearly demonstrated the authority that came from knowing who He was by not giving in to Satan's deceptions. You can read that account in Luke 4, but the outcome was that Satan realized he could not take Jesus' authority from Him.

Jesus would not relinquish His authority.

> *Now when the devil had ended every temptation, he departed from Him until an opportune time.-Luke 4:13*

Once Jesus had established His identity, He could begin to reveal His authority and purpose through His actions. This, as we now know, would mean great blessing for all mankind. Shortly after He defeated Satan, Jesus finally makes public His God ordained purpose by quoting Isaiah.

> *The Spirit of the Lord is upon Me, Because He has anointed Me to preach the gospel to the poor; He has sent Me to heal the brokenhearted, to proclaim liberty to the captives and recovery of sight to the blind, to set at liberty those who are oppressed; to proclaim the acceptable year of the Lord. - Luke 4:18-19*

Jesus accepted who He was, accepted that He would not let anything or anyone else tell Him who He was, and with that He was able to take all authority over this world and Satan's deceptions to the point of taking on and conquering death. Jesus, knowing who He was, ensured that He acted on His authority and with divine purpose.

Jesus knew that He would leave for us on earth the perfect example of how we should walk in our identity, authority and purpose. He said,

*These things I have spoken to you, that in Me you may have peace. In the world you will have tribulation; but be of good cheer, **I have overcome the world.**" - John 16:33 (emphasis mine)*

And then Jesus tells us what having authority and purpose can mean for us:

*Most assuredly, I say to you, he who believes in Me, the works that I do he will do also; **and greater works than these he will do**, because I go to My Father. - John 14:12 (emphasis mine)*

Walking in our identity, authority and purpose will ensure that we walk in the same power and direction that Jesus Christ did. It also means that we can affect change on a greater scale than even Jesus managed.

CHAPTER SEVEN
UNWRAPPED

"Greater love hath no man than this, that a man lay down his life for his friends." (John 15:13).

I love Christmas. Some of you may want to close the book right here because Christmas is not biblical and Jesus was not born in December. I don't care. I do Christmas—big time! Christmas is about my family and how much God loves us. Christmas for us is predictable and traditional. It rocks!

For us, Christmas usually starts with our Christmas gift distribution into any one of the communities our local church may be serving. South Africa is rich with possibilities where this tradition makes a huge impact. We do this all year round, but giving to those in need at Christmas is a little more special. And so it's become our tradition to find a small pocket of homeless people in our area and bless them extravagantly. Christmas cannot begin for me until I have spent time leading our family and some of the members of our church into an underprivileged area in our community.

Also, over the Christmas holidays, I get to play more golf than at any other time of the year, I spend loads of time building just about anything with Legos from the new gifts my children receive, and inevitably I walk away with a really neat new T-shirt. Apart from the community giving, however, the biggest kick I get out of Christmas is the fact that we open presents on Christmas Eve. I get to see my wife Leanne and my children opening their presents sooner rather than later. Every year I try to find a unique little gift for my wife that epitomizes the message in the card which always ends with: "Love you – Love me."

> *"For God so loved the world that He gave His only begotten Son, that whoever believes in Him should not perish but have everlasting life."- John 3:16*

These words could so easily be rewritten. "Hey Craig, I love you. - Love me". This always blows my mind. No matter how much I get to know Him, it amazes me that this scripture was not just referring to God loving the world collectively but that He loved you and me, individually. And that love is available to all.

God made His love available to every single human being. No discrimination.

"For there is no partiality with God." - Romans 2:11

It does not matter what set of legal or religious laws we may follow; God's grace is available to all. It's a gift placed under our Christmas tree just waiting to be unwrapped.

My Grandmother, who at the time of this writing is 93 years of age, taught me a valuable lesson as to the unwrapping of gifts we receive. She used to make a Sunday lunch that was just awesome. Her braised steak was one of the reasons why we love her. She is incredible in the kitchen. But she cooks old school style. We would buy her the latest appliances and kitchen gadgets to make her cooking life easier, but she would thank us and place the gift on top of the high cupboard in her kitchen. She never actually opened the boxes or used the gift. It would just sit there and never be used.

The gift of grace is often treated in the same way. God makes it available to us, but we often simply thank Him and store the gift in our intellect. We know He has given it, and we know that it's there, but we don't ever actually unwrap it and use it. Perhaps that's because we are still bound to believing in God's old school style; the God of wrath, laws and punishment.

So what is grace? What's in the unwrapped gift? There are two things we need to understand about this gift of grace, the first is what the gift is, and then more importantly what effect the gift has on our lives. Understanding the effect will not only give us reason to want to unwrap the gift, but it will also get us using it.

Let's take a look at the moment the gift of grace was given and maybe we can begin to better understand it.

*For God so loved the world that He **gave** His only begotten Son, that whoever believes in Him should not perish but have everlasting life. - John 3:16 (emphasis mine)*

The gift is Jesus. The story of Jesus is referred to as the "gospel." The first four books of the new testament—Matthew, Mark, Luke and John—are often called the gospels. They describe the arrival of the gift of grace on this earth in the form of Jesus Christ.

We could quite easily interchange the word grace and gospel. The word "gospel" in the Greek was not used very often at the time of the original writing of the gospels. It refers to something that was so incredible and awesome that there was little to compare it to. Gospel literally means "too good to be true news." At the time, with the persecution of the Christians and the slavery that came with their political situation, nothing was too good to be true, therefore the terminology had no point of reference.

Perhaps that's why many of us don't really appreciate the gift of the gospel. With all that goes on in our world, we don't really know how to respond to something that is too good to be true. Today we are up against so many empty promises and smashed hopes, that we are pushed to a place where even though we know it's grace, and we know it's the gospel, it just seems "too good to be true."

The apostle Paul began writing a whole series of books in the Bible (Romans, 1st & 2nd Corinthians, Galatians, Ephesians, Philippians Colossians, 1st & 2nd Thessalonians, 1st & 2nd Timothy, Titus and Philemon) after the gospels in an attempt to explain and to assure us that the gospels are indeed true.

> *For I am not ashamed of the gospel of Christ, **for it is the power of God to salvation for everyone who believes**, for the Jew first and also for the Greek. - Romans 1:16 (emphasis mine)*

The gospel, the gift of grace, is the power of God at work, saving everyone who believes. But saving us from what?—Our ordinary, everyday lives, our hurt and pain, the lies that we choose to believe about ourselves, the mediocrity of our lives and our lack of hope and purpose.

The gift of grace, however, does not stop there. Grace, in and of itself, does not fully describe the effect it has on our lives.

The first effect is that it unequivocally deepens our love for God. He made grace available to us even before we thought we needed it. He gave it to us when our lives were the furthest thing from Him. He knew it was for our good even when we didn't.

> *But God demonstrates His own love toward us, in that while we were still sinners, Christ died for us. - Romans 5:8*

Wow! While I was blaming God, while I was questioning His existence, while I was filling my life with lies, deceit and filth, He was placing gifts under my Christmas tree and hoping that one day I would read the card, open the gift and exercise my free will and choose His grace and use it for good.

I had become so accustomed to being rejected that I could not even begin to comprehend that there was this gift with my name on it waiting for me to unwrap it. How is that possible? It's called grace, and it's available to all of us.

Discovering grace made me realize that I could not sin grace away. While I was still living in sin, I learned that grace would always be there for me. The "power of God" trumped my sinful thoughts and actions. There is only one thing that could ever take me away from this blessed life of grace, and that is if I reverted to trusting in myself and my own 'good' deeds and not in God's "too good to be true" gift of grace.

And if by grace, then it is no longer of works; otherwise grace is no longer grace. But if it is of works, it is no longer grace; otherwise work is no longer work. - Romans 11:6

In fact, the acceptance we received through grace impels us to do good works. It is almost involuntary. Grace presses us to want to correct our sinful ways, to put down our bad habits and to bring our lives into line with the rest of what God asks of us. Good works are born from grace, we do not earn grace because of good works.

*For we are His workmanship, created in Christ Jesus **for good works**, which God prepared beforehand that we should walk in them. - Ephesians 2:10 (emphasis mine)*

There are some who feel that grace gives them license to do whatever they like and their behavior is always acceptable to God because of His gift of grace. Grace, however, is not a license to live life any which way we choose. We are to honor God's gift by our response to having received grace. It is a beautiful gift, and we dare not sully it with our former behavior.

Grace also does not mean that we are exempt from the consequences of our actions. It does not contradict the principle of sowing and reaping.

. . . A man reaps what he sows. Whoever sows to please their flesh, from the flesh will reap destruction;

whoever sows to please the Spirit, from the Spirit will reap eternal life" (Galatians 6:7-8).

Grace is God's constant offer to us that no matter what we are going through He loves us. Even when we make mistakes, God's power for our salvation still reigns supreme.

When we get it wrong we need to learn to change our response. We need to stop excusing, blaming and shaming and turn to the gift giver. Adam and Eve hid from God and were ashamed. Instead of stepping out from behind the bush and simply bending a knee and asking Him to forgive them, they allowed shame to trump grace. He was the one source that had their best interests at heart and would provide them with the best way forward, and yet they rejected Him. It was at that rejection of God by man that the effect of sin was brought upon humankind. *God never rejects us; we seek reasons to reject Him.*

The fact that He will not reject us, gives us a clear picture of how deep God's love is for us. As a result of His grace and that acceptance, we need to seek His principles in our lives. We cannot afford to fabricate our own preconceived solutions to our sin problem when grace is available to us all the time, every time.

CHAPTER EIGHT
BLIND FAITH

Now faith is the substance of things hoped for, the evidence of things not seen. - Hebrews 11:1

I was brought up a Jehovah's Witness and was trained weekly from a young age to go out and preach to others. Each month we were required to submit a report on our monthly activity. The report included the number of hours we spent preaching, the number of magazines and books we left with the public and whether or not we had revisited those we had previously spoken to.

The greater your activity, the more 'privileges' and responsibility you were assigned in the Jehovah's Witness organization. So from a young age I believed with all my heart that the more you do, the better you are. I also believed that the more I could achieve, the more faithful I was. God only saw me and was on my side if I was out there *doing* for the organization.

I was required to memorize the Jehovah's Witness training literature on how to counter objections and to reason from the scriptures with those we met. I carried with me a special briefcase in which I kept my 'stock' of magazines and books. As a fifteen year old I was out on the street preaching and sometimes volunteering up to 60 hours a month doing what is called 'field service.' By the time I left high school, however, I was disillusioned and tired of the hypocrisy I had experienced. I don't remember hearing from God or feeling Him in my life at all. I had *done* everything I was told would gain me God's approval. It was all about my personal report card; it had never occurred to me that I was out there to help others. I had always performed as instructed to gain the approval of my parents and others in my local congregation. To me God had become a distant report seeking god that only exacted my performance. I didn't believe that He was interested in me nor that he cared about me.

I began living the life that usually accompanies disillusionment, at least for me: No limitations, no moral code, no reports to submit and certainly no regard for the principles of God. The emptiness I felt grew. It drove me to try to prove myself in all the wrong ways. My life was in chaos which began to eat away at me. I could never be good enough, and I needed to do something about it, so I sought attention and acceptance from all the wrong places and people. I lied, cheated and manipulated my way into people's good opinions. Once they found out I was a fraud, they severed ties with me and left me even more depressed and disappointed with myself.

I was a mess. I so badly wanted to be good enough. I desperately needed to feel that I had purpose and meaning. I had made promises that I had no intention of keeping despite what everyone was thinking about me; I was going places, but I felt like a failure in every aspect of my life. My parents distanced themselves from me as I was an embarrassment to the organization and, therefore to them. Anger and rebellion became the order of the day for my life. At this point, I began to believe that God could not possibly exist and for me, the *story* of God was a fairy tale. Everything I had been taught was a lie to scare me into submission and to control me. I now hated God, whomever or whatever He was supposed to be.

It was by the grace of God that I met a very special women, Leanne, who would become my wife and who would change everything for me, even though I didn't know it at the time. That alone is another story well worth telling. But my life did radically change when, one day Leanne showed me a pink line on a home pregnancy test that announced I was to be a father.

When my son Kevin arrived, even before he could walk, he taught me more about my heavenly Father than I'd learned in my entire life. Although my own father hadn't been the best example for me, I wanted... no... needed to be a good dad. I wanted my son to trust me. I wanted him to know how much I loved him. I desperately wanted him to need me and love me back. I understood what it felt like to love my wife, but this was a different kind of love, one that I had never before experienced. I began to understand that if God was my Father as I had been told, then He must feel the same way toward me as I felt toward my son. As my Heavenly Father, He wanted me to love Him, and to trust Him even when I couldn't see Him or even if He hadn't yet made logical sense to me.

We each have a need, whether we admit it or not, to believe in something beyond ourselves, to dream and also to know that those dreams can be assured. That need is wired into each of us. As humans, we have an incredible ability to hope, despite all the facts and odds against us. Even though I had the wrong motivation initially, I had a driving desire to be able to hope that things could be better.

My hope, however, had always ended in disappointment. Sometimes my hope was dashed by decisions I had made and sometimes it was broken down by others in my life. When our hope is broken, passion drains from our lives. When the things we hope for never seem to materialize, no matter what we do, things get worse rather than better. Whatever light there may have been in our lives grows dim.

Hope deferred makes the heart sick, But when the desire comes, it is a tree of life. - Proverbs 13:12

I realized that I had always built my hope around my actions. I tried to take control of what my life should look like to protect myself from being too vulnerable should my dreams not come true. I wasn't about to allow anyone to hurt me again. I would never be taken as a fool with promises that if I did this or that then I would be a better person or would be able to sense God's approval. I wasn't seeking God's approval at all, I was seeking the approval of others and did things to try to gain it. No wonder I failed. What I was actually seeking was something I would later come to know and study called righteousness.

The Merriam-Webster Dictionary defines the word righteousness as *"acting in accord with divine or moral law: free from guilt, sin, hypocrisy: morally right or justifiable, arising from an outraged sense of justice or morality."* I began doing everything in my power to be right so that people would think I was good. The more I chased this hope of righteousness the more it alluded me. I wanted to be true to who I was and not be hypocritical. I wanted to be genuine. I still did not feel good enough. In fact, I no longer knew what I believed. I became a social chameleon. I became brilliant at fitting in with present company. It was easier to create a story, stretch the story and catch a bigger fish than admit to having caught nothing at all.

Nothing I ever did made me feel true, right and genuine. I always hoped I would find what I was looking for, but until my wife and I attended a small missions week at a local Methodist church, I didn't. There I read a scripture that I knew well, but that I had never heard with my heart.

Therefore, having been justified by faith, we have peace with God through our Lord Jesus Christ, through whom also we have access by faith into this grace in

which we stand, and rejoice in hope of the glory of God. And not only that, but we also glory in tribulations, knowing that tribulation produces perseverance; and perseverance, character; and character, **hope***. Now hope does not disappoint, because the love of God has been poured out in our hearts by the Holy Spirit who was given to us.*
- Romans 5:1-5 (emphasis mine)

The hope that I already had in my heart simply had to be redirected. I had not been made right or justified by the things I did and would never have found peace had I not opened my heart to the Word. I learned that I did not have to become anything I wasn't. It was through this thing called faith that character, perseverance and hope is produced. And this new kind of hope would not disappoint me or anyone.

For by grace you have been saved through faith, and that not of yourselves; it is the gift of God . . .
- Ephesians 2:8

Faith is not simply hoping and wishing on what we do, it is faith in Jesus Christ alone. *Faith is a position of our hearts.* It is a decision to believe completely, to devote ourselves to discovering more of Christ each day. It is believing without evidence, losing ourselves in God's wonderful grace and Jesus Christ. We don't need a fossil record to prove that what we believe is right.

Now faith is the substance of things hoped for, the evidence of things not seen. - Hebrews 11:1

Faith *is* the evidence. Faith *is* the substance. It is *not* a search or a quest. When we place our faith is Christ, we arrive, we are accepted and need not add one more thing to the equation for it to be true. As Christ declares in John 19: "It is done."

Now may the God of hope fill you with all joy and peace in believing, that you may abound in hope by the power of the Holy Spirit. - Romans 15:13

When we accept the concept of God's grace into our lives, that faith, like unpacking a suitcase, begins to unfold incredible truths that we have always hoped for in our lives but could not accomplish on our own. We not only receive the hope we had longed for, but faith moves into our hearts. Finding faith in Christ means that we now have heart based evidence of Him conquering the grave. That means the eternity God wired into us as a hope, has now become a reality.

He has made everything beautiful in its time. **Also He has put eternity in their hearts,** *except that no one can find out the work that God does from beginning to end. - Ecclesiastes 3:11 (emphasis mine)*

When the hope of our minds meets the faith of our heart, miracles happen. When I discovered the miracle that eternity awaited me and was in fact a reality in my life on earth, it gave me a peace that changed my life. My newfound faith in Jesus Christ gave birth to a personal and cherished peace in my spirit, which had, without Christ, been in constant turmoil. Faith in Christ had given birth to peace.

Faith is a decision. It is not a mental decision or an academic one, but it is a heart decision and one that as Christians we long to keep even when our lives don't seem to be filled with the blessings and the miracles we seek.

Despite difficulties, faith always bears fruit. Once you comprehend that Christ is yours, you will want to celebrate that faith by doing something about it. Our faith is not a result of deeds, it is a result of celebrating our faith by doing something to honor God, even when to do so is difficult. Difficulties and challenges can cause us to doubt our faith and doubt is the enemy of faith.

We must stay focused on the love of Jesus Christ which resides within us to avoid succumbing to doubt.

For he who doubts is like a wave of the sea driven and tossed by the wind. - James 1:6

We must put our faith in God and allow that faith to infiltrate our decision making or we are going to lose that peace and become unsettled or worse yet, give a foothold to the enemy who only desires to rob, steal and destroy our peace. God loves us and simply wants us to believe in the grace solution He has provided. With it, every blessing and miracle, every promise and dream that He desires for us becomes not only evident but possible.

As humans with a choice, some of us have an incredible ability to find every possible reason not to believe. Just like Adam and Eve, we seem to doubt all too easily, and we like to create excuses to justify our position. "I am not good enough," or "God could never love me." "I can't get past what he/she did to me", or, like a spoiled child, "God let me down when he didn't give me my way." And so the excuses come. But there is a source that we can stand upon that will always build faith and trump our excuses and doubt.

So then faith comes by hearing, and hearing by the word of God. - Romans 10:17

We need to believe what the Bible tells us about ourselves rather than allow doubts and deceptions to shake our faith. When we open our hearts to what scripture tells us, our faith begins to grow and those blessings promised in scripture become our reality. Not the reality as we see it, but the reality as God sees it.

God would rather we love Him and trust Him enough to blindly believe His promises (faith) than to wander with no direction, no peace and be ruled by doubt.

CHAPTER NINE
BLESSED

The Lord will open to you His good treasure, the heavens, to give the rain to your land in its season, and to bless all the work of your hand. You shall lend to many nations, but you shall not borrow. - Deuteronomy 28:12

God's principle of being blessed has been distorted more by the Christian church than by anyone or anything else. In fact when we mention the word 'blessed' in many Christian circles, images of a preacher ranting and raving about prosperity usually come to mind. We have monetized blessings and distorted them to mean *financial prosperity*. We have turned it into a transaction. "Give and God will multiply your finances."(so that we can pay for the rantings of that prosperity preacher.)

Please understand that I am not about to negate the teaching of blessing and prosperity in the Bible. Both of these principles are found in scripture. However, living God's principle of blessing means so much more than some have made it out to be.

Before we begin to understand what it means to be blessed, we must understand what it does not mean. To do that, forgive me if we quickly put some "sacred cows" out to pasture.

It is not about financial prosperity alone. It is not walking around in a super spiritual state of bliss, oblivious to the issues and problems of the world. It is not found in anointing your new home with oil, or blowing a shofar. It does not come from the sprinkling of water or through performing a series of religious rituals. Certain people are not more blessed than others, and we certainly don't need to live life piggy-backing on someone else's blessing and anointing. You will not lead a blessed life because of the preaching of a pastor or the waving around of a healing cloth.

Some of these actions or beliefs are in fact found in the Bible and the practice of them is not necessarily wicked or wrong. But in such practices we have created the criteria that informs us whether or not we are blessed. Let's say a friend comes into some money or gets the dream job. We automatically think that they are more blessed than someone who may be struggling to make ends meet. We believe that the people living in the rural setting such as Blantyre, Malawi cannot possibly be as blessed as those who live in the United States because they don't have as many material things.

We have created our own set of criteria that must be present if we are to be blessed, and we have lost track of what God meant when He blessed the human race in Eden, when He blessed us again on Golgotha and when He blessed us with the sending of His Holy Spirit and certainly all of His future blessings.

The very first time the Bible mentions God blessing anyone, is found in the scripture that tells us of God setting man and women in place on earth. Let's take a close look at the unveiling of this first blessing. It will give us an understanding of what it genuinely looks like to be blessed.

As we have learned He first made us in His image (Chapter Five).

Then God said, "Let Us make man in Our image, according to Our likeness; - Genesis 1:26a

Then once He had made us in His image, He established our authority over the earth (Chapter Six).

> *...let them have **dominion** over the fish of the sea, over the birds of the air, and over the cattle, over all the earth and over every creeping thing that creeps on the earth. - Genesis 1:26b (emphasis mine)*

Having been made in God's image, we have also received the ability to govern over the earth (dominion). This governance is based on God's Word and principles and not our own. But because we are godlike (made in his image) we have this power only when we submit to His authority. The scripture in Genesis clearly identifies how God set us up, how He wired it all together for our benefit. First He gave us an identity by making us in His image. Then He gave us authority over the earth and finally blessed humankind.

Let's read the whole scripture again and see those three elements of our wiring coming together.

> *Then God said, "**Let Us make man in Our image**, according to Our likeness; **let them have dominion** over the fish of the sea, over the birds of the air, and over the cattle, over all the earth and over every*

*creeping thing that creeps on the earth." So God created man in His own image; in the image of God He created him; male and female He created them. **Then God blessed them**, and God said to them, "Be fruitful and multiply; fill the earth and subdue it; have dominion over the fish of the sea, over the birds of the air, and over every living thing that moves on the earth." - Genesis 1:26-28 (Emphasis mine)*

Being made in His image and being wired like Him is important in understanding Gods blessings in our lives. The blessing comes from our identity in Christ and the resultant authority that we have been given. We cannot just jump in and claim blessings without walking in the authority and the identity that He has given us. All three work together.

We mirror who He is. God is a three part being: God the Father, God the Son and God the Holy Spirit. It stands to reason then that if God is a three part being, and we are made in His image, then we too are three part beings. Our structure, DNA and lives are governed by three parts.

*Now may the God of peace Himself sanctify you completely; and may your whole **spirit, soul, and body** be preserved blameless at the coming of our Lord Jesus Christ. - 1 Thessalonians 5:23 (emphasis mine)*

We have a spirit, a soul and a body. That is our image. When we begin to operate in an understanding of what this means, we begin to understand that we have authority in this world. We reflect every part of God. We can operate with confidence in every one of His qualities. We are not defined by this broken world, but reflect a perfect heavenly Father. Simply being made in His image is a blessing. Being able to operate in divine authority is a blessing. No wonder God declares humankind blessed.

> **Then God blessed them**, *and God said to them, "Be fruitful and multiply; fill the earth and subdue it; have dominion over the fish of the sea, over the birds of the air, and over every living thing that moves on the earth." - Genesis 1:28 (emphasis mine)*

When we accept our identity and authority, it pleases God to see us operating in the way that He wired us. He knows that the combination of our authority and identity will always result in blessings. When we do these things, God is well pleased and He can rest in the assurance that His will for us is being accomplished. He declares this state of humankind good.

> *Then God saw everything that He had made,* ***and indeed it was very good****. So the evening and the*

morning were the sixth day. - Genesis 1:31 *(emphasis mine)*

This was just the first description in the Bible of the blessings that the Father had in mind for me. I began a search not to find the blessings promised but to find the principles that relate to my identity and authority so that I could implement them in my life. I wanted to please the Father that had laid so much on the line to make sure I would live a life of blessing.

Knowing that I could find blessing by simply living out the principles of God and that those principles were meticulously spelled out for me in the Word of God, I decided that the Bible would become my *go to* for everything in my life. I was already passionate about the Bible, and now knowing that God had laid out all His principles and thus all His blessings in it, I wanted to consume every word. I was not searching for the blessing, I was searching for the love of my God.

Experiencing the blessings meant that I had to learn His principles. I had to be committed to studying His Word. The more I studied, the more overwhelmed I became with His principles. I was awestruck as the full revelation of "God is love" was made real to me. "God is love" is a profound principle of God. He cannot change that. This principle governs His actions. So when things are going badly, we can be blessed with the knowledge that our situation does not change the principle of "God is love" to "God is hate." It cannot be changed. Knowing that principle brings about such a peace—a blessing in itself.

Is this easier said than done? When we experience the trials that we are dealt by life, it becomes more difficult to focus on God's principles, let alone remember how we have been blessed through them. One of the other principles that I hold onto when the going gets tough is the principle of eternity. Regardless of what this world delivers right now, our eternity remains. The security we have in knowing that God has no end and that He gives eternity to all those who believe in Him means that we have been blessed with a courage and a fortitude to press on, fight the fight and run the race. Nothing, not even death can separate us from the love of God.

> *And I am convinced that nothing can ever separate us from God's love. Neither death nor life, neither angels nor demons, neither our fears for today nor our worries about tomorrow—not even the powers of hell can separate us from God's love. No power in the sky above or in the earth below—indeed, nothing in all creation will ever be able to separate us from the love*

of God that is revealed in Christ Jesus our Lord. Romans 8:38-39

With the knowledge that not even death could rob me of an eternal life with God, I found that I had a peace that birthed in me an inner strength that I had not known before. If death itself had no power over me, what else could I accomplish with the strength of Christ?

I can do all things through Christ who strengthens me. - Philippians 4:13

Once we understand that we have been given genuine authority over this life, we have discovered our greatest blessing. Our situations and our issues do not define who we are. We have been defined by God as eternal spirit beings that He loves unconditionally. Far too often, the word blessing has been translated to mean something physical, something we can own. But the blessing of God is all about knowing who and what we are through Him. When we get to know Him through His principles as laid out in scripture, we gain a life we could never imagine on our own. Not only an eternal life but a life that not even difficulties like stress or cancer can threaten. It's His peace, joy and confidence that helps us to always transcend what we face in our lives.

The real blessing is in understanding what God has truly blessed us with and not in material possessions. *The blessing is in the knowing and not the having.*

*And this is eternal life, that they may **know** You, the only true God, and Jesus Christ whom You have sent. - John 17:3 (emphasis mine)*

When we walk through life with an understanding of God's principles and their effects on our lives, we begin to see things differently. *Knowing* we have eternity changes our perspective on everything. *Knowing* we are His children, dispels our sense of loneliness, rejection or abandonment. *Knowing* that He wants us physically well and that it is this broken world that causes disease and illness and not God, gives us strength to face physical infirmities. *Knowing* that His love is so abundant changes our desire and need to do things to earn His favor. And so we could go on. To walk on this earth in a blessed state, all we need to know is what His promises and principles are. We need to believe those promises as unbreakable and fit for every situation. We need to speak them at all times, knowing that doubt is right there waiting to rob steal and destroy.

The thief does not come except to steal, and to kill, and to destroy. I have come that they may have life, and that they may have it more abundantly. - John 10:10

Knowing allows peace to prevail in our lives and gives us margin to make better decisions, to endure more and to declare good in our lives over depression and malediction. I have come to realize that as long as I embrace God's peace and love, this life has no power over me and cannot destroy me. I have authority over this life, and since I know this, I can walk in the blessing of His peace and love. It is not a new car or a great job that makes me blessed, it's knowing Him. Knowing His love and sensing Him walking beside me and living in me every moment of every day.

Blessed be the God and Father of our Lord Jesus Christ, who has blessed us with every spiritual blessing in the heavenly places in Christ, - Ephesians 1:3

Once we believe, we have already received every spiritual blessing we need. We don't have to beg God because His answer remains constant. "It is done."

I have heard the line, "I am waiting on God," many times. Waiting for what? Are we waiting for God to implement a new principle or blessing? God does not have new solutions to old problems. Why do we wait on

Him when He has already established every principle and blessing we need? Every one of God's principles carries with it a blessing that has already been put in place. He does not need to come up with new principles or change who He is to find ways to bless us. Our blessings and His principles are entwined with who He is. He has no beginning or end and as such neither do His principles or our blessings.

The blessings from God have already been provided. He does not need to miraculously step into every situation. He has already provided the principles that govern everything and that unlock blessings. When we know this, we should expect to see His blessings in our lives rather than be begging and pleading for a miracle. Even if we are in a situation that makes it very difficult to see this practically, what we must remember is that He has already provided everything we need.

Far too often we allow this life to dictate to us how we feel and what we believe. We should rather decide what we believe and then live our lives accordingly. We have been given authority. We have been made in His image. We have already been blessed. These are the principles that should guide our lives not our feelings or emotions.

We must believe with all of our being that God has already poured out His love through Jesus Christ and that we are lovingly guided by the Holy Spirit.

Now hope does not disappoint, because the love of God has been poured out in our hearts by the Holy Spirit who was given to us. - Romans 5:5

God is constantly blessing us whether we *feel* it or not. His love has been poured into our hearts. It isn't conditionally based on our good behavior, holiness or being at the right place at the right time. We have already been given the potential to walk daily in God's blessing.

Consider this. When you **know** that you already have something, it takes the stress and the wrestle out of obtaining it. It's the same with God's blessings, we don't have to work or even try to win them. They become ours when we declare Christ in our lives. We automatically and immediately walk in His blessings.

All we need to do is believe that those blessings are ours, even though we can't see, taste, hear, smell, or feel them as we as humans tend to expect. We just need to know Him, and knowing His principles makes sure that the very best is deposited into our lives.

He will not leave us short, He can't. To leave us out of His blessings goes against everything He is. Once we are His, He refuses to do eternity without us!

CHAPTER TEN
TRUE NORTH

Where there is no purpose, people cast off restraint; but blessed is the one who heeds wisdom's instruction. - Proverbs 29:18

When I was working on the outline for this book and wrestling with titles and theme verses for each chapter, I decided on Proverbs 29:18 for this chapter and never doubted it for a moment. I knew that this would be the most exciting chapter for me to write. Finding one's purpose in life is my favorite subject to speak or write about.

I have dabbled in the theatre for as far back as I can remember. From amateur acting to professional lighting and sound, I love the theatre. The very first professional production I ever attended was a performance of Peter Pan in a theatre in Rondebosch Cape Town, South Africa. It was called the Baxter Theatre and even though I was only 7 years old, I vowed that one day I would work in the Baxter. I watched actors flying around, hoisted into the air by cables, and I was lost, not in the world of Neverland, but in the world of stagecraft. I focused on the fly bars. lighting systems, set changes and costumes. As Peter chased his shadow across the stage, I noted that they used a fine black mesh on a cable pulley system as his shadow. As Tinkerbell fluttered past, I got my first look at a lighting mechanism called a gobo. (You can wiki that.) I was enthralled by "how they did that."

Many years later, I would return as a sound technician to the ballet company that performed at the Baxter Theatre. By the time I returned I had participated in many other productions on and off stage. I even won some stage play writing awards in my High School years. I was the chairman of my High School Drama Society and won many honors and awards because of the theatre.

The biggest moment in my theatrical experiences came when I was directing a rock opera called TEN. It was a stage play I had written and with the help of many talented musicians and performers, I was blessed to see the production take to the stage four times.

The production told the story of Moses, a humble, poor spoken man who was trying to free his people against the backdrop of the all-powerful Egyptian empire and its charismatic Pharaoh. I made a director's decision to spend many long hours directing a young man named Mitch who was to play Pharaoh. I believed that the more I could help him act out this all powerful self-proclaimed god, the more it would highlight Moses' humility and timidity and thus demonstrate how much God's hand was in liberating the Israelites.

There came a moment during rehearsal when I leapt onto the stage in an effort to demonstrate to some other actors what the appropriate response to one of Pharaoh's quips should be. Half way through my recitation of Pharaoh's lines, I realized that I was not performing the role nearly as well as Mitch had performed it. He had cracked the code and had made the role his own. I may have birthed the role in my fertile imagination based on scripture, but he had mastered it far better than I could.

If you're reading this Mitch, it was in that moment, unbeknownst to you, that a purpose stirred in me, one that still sets my course today. When I can help someone do something better than I can, I come alive. My passion and my purpose has become to empower others to lead and to embrace Christ and to grow in leadership in a way that far surpasses even their own expectations. I live for the moment when the pupil becomes the teacher. I find myself purposely seeking out the "underdog." Over the years this simple truth has become evident to me; *I have yet to see anyone who inspires others to greatness not go onto greatness themselves.*

So how do we discover our purpose?

I have taken many spiritual gift tests and character assessments and usually get the same results. Assessments are wonderful tools to help direct us toward what role we should play in this world. They are tools that provide a very good understanding of what our purpose is, what our gifts and talents are and what we are generally good at. Maybe you rank highly as an encourager or you can administrate well. Whatever the outcome, these assessments seldom indicate to us the *why* behind the *what*.

It dawned on me that the *what* is simply the fruit of the *why*. What I mean by that is we often know what we are good at. We may not think what we are good at is really good at all, but some things still feel more natural to us than others. Understanding *why* we show a leaning toward one area of the gift assessment helps us to understand that we have a very unique *why* motivating *what* we do. In an incredible small groups course offered by LifeChurch, Oklahoma called Chazown (by Craig Groeschel and available at www.chazown.com) I learned that my higher ranking abilities or talents were all present because of my past experiences. Having been an outcast as a little boy struggling with epilepsy made me appreciate and respect society's less fortunate. Every *what* in my life had a *why* and that *why* was unique to me. No one else could possess exactly the same life experiences that lead toward my becoming an encourager. Many others may also have encourager be the result of their assessment as their top *what* but no one else could have the exact same story behind *why* encourager came out on top for me.

I got a kick out of seeing the student become the teacher, and no one else on this planet can get to that place in exactly the same way I did. I am unique! It stands to reason then that if I am unique to my strengths because of my experiences, then there are unique situations in which I would be able to provide something invaluable to others. I had a purpose.

The Chazown study also highlighted that many of the motivations behind my strengths, came from moments of pain in my life. The areas of my life that I would rather hide and forget were actually the impetus toward creating purpose in my life.

That's why I take pleasure in my weaknesses, and in the insults, hardships, persecutions, and troubles that I suffer for Christ. **For when I am weak, then I am strong.** *- 2 Corinthians 12:10 (emphasis mine)*

I began to understand that this scripture did not just mean that I could overcome difficulties but that in my weakest moments, the moments in my past that caused the greatest pain, were actually directly related to shaping my unique and meaningful purpose in this world.

To take that a step further, when we allow Christ to shape our weaknesses He can turn them into our greatest assets. When we allow His Word and His Wisdom to decipher the difficulties in our lives, it will always result in our good. By allowing His incredible and unique understanding of who we are and His love for us to always be on the forefront of our minds, He can transform the hurt and the pain into something beneficial and positive. It's why we, as Christians, can say that He bore our pain at the cross. There will be hurts and there will be pain, but because of Christ's incredible act of love we can see pain transformed to joy and hopelessness transformed to purpose. Once we have a purpose, we can have hope, and when we have hope, faith abounds.

Faith is the confidence that what we hope for will actually happen; it gives us assurance about things we cannot see. Hebrews 11:1

We cannot know what will happen tomorrow, but if we allow the transforming act of love by Jesus Christ to turn our weaknesses into a confidence by accepting Him as our Savior, that act alone gives birth to hope, not hate or hurt, and we can begin to discover our unique purpose that is based on faith, hope and love.

And now these three remain: faith, hope and love. But the greatest of these is love. 1 Corinthians 13:13

God has placed in us a desire to have a purpose. He knows that for us to be able to hold onto faith, hope and love and not let doubt and anger rob us of all we can be, that we would need to have something to do. He knows that if we feel like we have a unique contribution to make that we would be more prone to make that contribution rather than give up and be defeated without it. He also placed in us a desire for our purpose to be a positive one. That's the God He is. He also loves it when the servant becomes the master. Historically in scripture, He's done it time and time again—out of weakness is born greatness.

> *At that time I will gather you; at that time I will bring you home. I will give you honor and praise among all the peoples of the earth when I restore your fortunes before your very eyes," says the LORD. - Zephaniah 3:20*

God beheld a weak, timid, embarrassed little man named Gideon and called him a mighty warrior. He heard Moses refer to himself as poor of speech and gave him the power to become one of the greatest freedom speakers of all time. He chose a barren women and saw to it that the savior of all mankind came from her offspring. He hand-picked a ridiculed and mocked man and instructed him to build an ark. He can take us and turn our every weakness into a strength, every discomfort into comfort and hope and every disappointment into purpose. God can make the dead live again. He spoke everything into being from nothing and we can trust Him to take our hurts and make them powerful forces for His glory. He has both the ability to create and transform. He creates something out of nothing and can transform nothing into something.

So you believe you are a nothing. Any one of us can ask God to turn that nothing into something right now. We each have a unique purpose and are destined for greatness once we discover our purpose and put it to use—not greatness that is based on wealth or worldly success, but greatness based on faith, hope and love.

Your greatest weakness is exactly where, with Jesus' help, you can find your greatest passion.

That is what the Scriptures mean when God told him, "I have made you the father of many nations." This happened because Abraham believed in the God who brings the dead back to life and who creates new things out of nothing. - Romans 4:17

God took Adam and Eve, made them in His image, gave them authority and blessed them, but He also gave them a purpose. He gave them the tools and then He told them what they were to do with them.

Then God blessed them and said, "Be fruitful and multiply. Fill the earth and govern it. Reign over the fish in the sea, the birds in the sky, and all the animals that scurry along the ground." Genesis 1:28

Adam and Eve woke up every morning and knew *what* they were to do because in their heart they had a *why*. They had been commissioned by the Most High God Himself. They would bring Him glory and honor and they would worship Him because of the love that had been lavished on them. They were to do this with authority, blessing and purpose.

All that we are and all that we hope to become is so vitally important to us because we have a principle placed in our hearts by God Himself. He wants us to lift ourselves from our current situation and to achieve with a purpose. He wants us to cry out joyfully because we have not allowed the difficulties of life to be victorious over us but have rather got something meaningful to do. However small our purpose may seem to us in the greater scheme of things, it is not our achievement or anything we do that makes Him proud. What makes God proud is when, because it has been against all odds and has been from a place of weakness, we give Him the honor for what we achieve. Our deep-seated hurts sometimes cloud our beliefs and make us believe that we cannot achieve anything meaningful. Even though we often doubt our abilities because of previous disappointments, God is still waiting for us to take a small step towards our purpose, find it and celebrate with Him. When we celebrate with Him that leads to our being motivated and once we are motivated, we can become unconquerable. It stirs in us a desire to move from one challenge to the next, to stretch ourselves and, with the power we have inside, to stare down doubt and to become aware of what we can do and how we can uniquely build a world for ourselves that celebrates love and joy and not pain and hurt.

God introduced prophets into the nation of Israel to help them understand that if they did not embrace their purpose their future would be bleak to say the least. God sent prophets to tell the nations who failed to embrace His love and direction of what their future would look like.

We sometimes wish that someone would come along and give us a 'prophetic word' now and again – just like the prophets of old. Someone that we could trust that would unlock our purpose and, as a result, reveal our future. We do gift assessments in an attempt to gain enlightenment or revelation of our purpose and thus what our future holds. We seek those who seem to "flow" in this gift of the prophetic who say things like: "The Lord is saying to you that you are gifted with children and you will minister to many thousands of children." Don't get me wrong, I believe in words of wisdom and knowledge and that God can use others to guide and lead us. The point I am trying to make is that revelation, prophecy and God's Word are entwined into our journey of purpose discovery.

Where there is no purpose, people cast off restraint; but blessed is the one who heeds wisdom's instruction.
- Proverbs 29:18

When we heed God's words of love and His blessing and direction, we begin to understand how He can use our weaknesses to build strength in us. It is only by His word that we can make that miraculous transformation. We need to immerse ourselves in His Word and His instruction to obtain the desired result. Just like with Adam and Eve, He speaks of our purpose and warns that should we listen to any other word of instruction as to what our future and purpose might look like, we will find only disillusionment and disappointment. He alone is the creator of our purpose. Seek Him and you will find direction. Heed his Wisdom and unwrap the blessings that await.

CHAPTER ELEVEN
PHOTO ALBUM

... that this may be a sign among you when your children ask in time to come, saying 'What do these stones mean to you?' Joshua 4:6

As a young boy, I loved photography. I would spend hours ogling over equipment in the local photographic store—the kind of equipment I knew I would probably never be able to afford.

I eventually saved enough money to purchase a small 35mm camera. It wasn't anything fancy, but it allowed me to attach some flash units, a tripod and at least to feel like I had the best camera setup in the world. The truth of it was that when the time came to snap the perfect picture, I could never trust that it would turn out exactly as I wanted it. It was pre-digital photography. I used spools of 35mm film that would have to be sent into a local lab for developing. If you don't know what I am talking about, you are probably of the Instagram and digital camera generation. I wasted a lot of money developing pictures that were over-exposed or a blur, but even those blurry, bright orange photographs, held some form of a memory. I would hold onto what I could remember of the image that I had tried to capture so that regardless of the picture quality, I could at least attempt to make out what it was I had been trying to photograph. The waiting and anticipation of the next set of prints, which hopefully would contain a brilliantly taken photograph, kept me going. Regardless of quality, call me sentimental, I kept them all. The good ones, as few as they were, and the bad ones, more than I want to admit.

Every picture had a thought behind it. Every print had been initiated with a purpose. Slowly the number of bad prints got fewer and fewer and eventually I began to take some pretty good pictures. But every now and then, when I rushed to collect my next set of prints from the local photo lab, I would still find blurry, orange photos. In retrospect, it's what kept me photographically humble.

Years went by and I discovered that not all of life can be photographed. My life began developing memories that could not be captured on film or even on Instagram but which were indelibly etched into my memory. Events, people and emotions would burn images into my imagination that would begin to shape me into who I was, how I would react to situations and what my core values would become. Whether I wanted to or not, I had to keep all of these images stored away in the recesses of my mind. The mental images of being rejected alongside images of being accepted. The blurry orange of hurt alongside the clear images of hope.

Perhaps your mental album is like mine, full of blurry orange memories rather than perfect images. Whatever the ratio of good to bad imagery, every one of those mental photographs carries a very vivid memory: some capture and preserve the lows while others the highs of our lives.

As I began to realize that God's design and image was wired into me and I allowed it to be developed, I began making better decisions, no matter the situation. I began to develop some pretty good mental images. The memory of the image may still have been painful, but the reason for the situation and the effect it had on me all became clearer. I deliberately made sure to remember things in a way that would teach me, grow me and allow me to be more obedient to God, more tolerant and loving of others and above all, in a way that would always find God's love in everything.

Memories of my childhood were the orange burry type. More hurt than joy and loads more conflict than I want to remember. But knowing that God was wired into me even through those very painful and hurtful years, I am now able to look at those photographs and see clearly how God was developing in me a desire to be a better father and husband, how he was building in me a desire to passionately take the Gospel to the world and to back the underdog. In those mental pictures I saw that God always seemed to photo bomb all my pictures with His love and passion for me.

You may have to hunt, squint and really look hard sometimes, but you must never believe that any mental photo of your life is devoid of God's love. He may not have caused a situation or pain, but His presence in those moments is undeniable.

God is not in the business of bad and sad. He is in the business of working for the good in every situation.

And we know that God causes everything to work together for the good of those who love God and are called according to his purpose for them. - Romans 8:28

I recall hearing a story about a group of friends that illustrates this best. These friends were discussing a terrible motor vehicle accident that had occurred along a notorious stretch of road in the area in which they lived. It had been the fifth accident on this road that month.

One of them blurted out. "I know who causes these accidents."

Everyone looked at him a little confused. "You know who causes every one of these accidents?" asked another.

"Yes", the man replied. "It's very obvious. It's the police".

The others were even more confused.

"How do you even begin to explain that idea?" one friend asked.

"Easy, the police are at every one of the accidents.

You see them there every time. It must be them; they are the only common denominator."

"That's no reason to blame the police for causing accidents. They are there to help," replied the man's closest friend.

My point is that just because we know that God is ever present, that does not mean He is to be blamed when things go badly in our lives. He is there to help.

As I look back through my mental photo album, I can see Him clearly in all the images in my mind. At the time, and even as time separated me from the actual event, I may not have been able to make head or tail of Him in anything. But as I got to know who He was, as I discovered His immense love and began to live my life in His image, I began to recognize His presence everywhere and in everything. I often revisit the mental photographs of the past. The ones I took before I knew Him as well as how I know Him today. I have always been able to find Him in those pictures. He was never causing the hurt, but He was always there to help.

For example, I recall a time when at 5 years old, I was standing in a tweed suit giving a talk in front of a Jehovah's Witness congregation. I was terrified that I would not do it exactly like my father had instructed me. God was preparing me for ministry done the right way, His way. In the photos of my rejection through junior school, I see God preparing my heart to become a voice for the down trodden. What about that one of when my father had cruelly beaten me, and I had to hide the cuts with bandages and make up stories of what happened when I went to school. There He was, teaching me the value of being a good father to my children.

That's why I take pleasure in my weaknesses, and in the insults, hardships, persecutions, and troubles that I suffer for Christ. For when I am weak, then I am strong. - 2 Corinthians 12:10

It is not just about finding a silver lining in every cloud. No, it is finding the God who we've learned loves us completely in whatever situation. It is understanding that we have a choice regardless of how bad the circumstances. In such a photographic moment, we must choose to respond either in a way that shows we love Him, or in a way that demonstrates we are governed by the lies that Satan is trying to make us believe. It is just his attempt to steal our joy. But if we choose to find and honor God's love, we will be obedient to His principles and, as a result, the blessings of His promises will become reality.

The thief's purpose is to steal and kill and destroy. My purpose is to give them a rich and satisfying life. - John 10:10

The highs or lows of life and the situations we find ourselves in often distorts our vision and blurs our ability to seek His love, trust Him enough to obey His principles and to receive His blessings. We can sometimes feel like we are on an emotional rollercoaster. We feel that we are completely disconnected from Him. He could never be in us. Our lives don't look like we are connected to Him and that He is wired into us. *Having a memory of Him working in our lives, pulls us back from denying His existence during our hurt.*

That's the benefit of taking spiritual photos. Remembering a scripture that helped you recognize the presence of God in a certain mental image may help you later when you feel blurred and orange.

We blow about like flowers in the breeze, but when we study and know Him, we can set our gaze confidently and firmly on the future. No longer do we need to be blown about by how we feel about our past—situations that may once have left us throwing our hands up and blaming God. They now become reasons to believe, to know that we have a better future and we are not defined by our past. *Our image is in Him not in our hurt.*

The grass withers and the flowers fall, because the breath of the LORD blows on them. Surely the people are grass. The grass withers and the flowers fade, but the word of our God stands forever. - Isaiah 40:7-8

When on one of life's highs, we need to stop, take a look around and post as many pictures to our mental timeline as we can. Check the disciplines you are engaging in, the food you are eating, the amount of time you are spending reading the Bible, the scriptures that got you on the high in the first place, the people you were associating with (*Do not be misled: "Bad company corrupts good character."* 1 Corinthians 15:33), what aspects of God seemed the most real, how much time you are spending with your family, which principles of God are most applicable, etc, etc. Take whatever mental photographs you need to make sure you have a clear image of Him during that time. You will be amazed when you hit the inevitable lows and the valleys. Take out your photo album, and remember. You can see God right there at the bottom of the worst day during the heaviest storm. It might be blurry, but when you focus on the clear image of the God that you serve and that you know, no matter the situation, you are now able to choose life not death.

> *Every valley shall be raised up, every mountain and hill made low; the rough ground shall become level, the rugged places a plain. Isaiah 40:4*

Facebook makes it possible to make a video from all of the pictures you have posted during the past year. It creates a memory view of what and who you were posting about. After nearly a year of ministry travel with my family through the United States, I ran the Facebook tool and made a video of all our pictures. As each photo I had selected came up with music and captions added, I realized that each of those pictures had an individual story to tell, but when placed together they told a collective story about a courageous family on a mission with God. From all the memories came a single theme, a revelation.

By snapping those mental pictures and seeing how God has wired them all together, we create moments of revelation. Every now and then we say things like *"God has a sense of humor,"* or *"I didn't understand why He did that, but looking back on it I can see what He was doing."* These moments generally mark the times in our journey when solutions to problems become apparent or a light can be seen at the end of the proverbial tunnel. These are the moments when we recognize God in our reality because of that revelation. He has in a mighty way transformed the immediate problem and then magnanimously and miraculously rippled solutions and growth through other areas of our spiritual existence. Once we begin to have these revelation moments, they affect every photograph we have ever taken, whether good or bad, transforming them and our lives more and more into the glorious image of Him.

Please don't wait to start your photo album. Use that journal that has been sitting on your desk or in a box for years or open a new note on whatever digital device you may own. Begin capturing God's love in the photo moments of your life. Become a master at identifying Him in them all. He is there ready to reveal His love to you. He wants you to love Him, trust Him, obey Him. Remember, He wants to bless you.

CHAPTER TWELVE
THE END OF IT ALL

The thief does not come except to steal, and to kill, and to destroy. I have come that they may have life, and that they may have it more abundantly. - John 10:10

Even as God's children, we must admit that we can make some pretty rank and strange decisions. We take on the decision making process by weighing right against wrong. We were not wired for this process. Our choices were only ever supposed to be between right and right and never wrong and right. Okay, now that you are totally confused, let me tell you *why* and *how*.

Satan asked Adam and Eve questions that shook their trust in God and the choices He had laid out for them. It wasn't long before they felt that God's ways might not result in what was best for them and that on their own they could do better.

> *The serpent was the shrewdest of all the wild animals the* LORD *God had made. One day he asked the woman, "Did God really say you must not eat the fruit from any of the trees in the garden?"*
>
> *"Of course we may eat fruit from the trees in the garden," the woman replied. "It's only the fruit from the tree in the middle of the garden that we are not allowed to eat. God said, 'You must not eat it or even touch it; if you do, you will die.'"*
>
> *"You won't die!" the serpent replied to the woman. "God knows that your eyes will be opened as soon as you eat it, and you will be like God, knowing both good and evil." – Genesis 3:1-5*

Once Satan had caused doubt and had broken the trust that Adam and Eve had in God, obedience to Him no longer seemed like their best and only option. They believed that their new way of thinking would bring greater blessings. Satan lured them into believing that the true, optimal ways of God may not be the best way for them. Against God's instruction, they ate of the tree of the knowledge of good and evil. This disobedience began the debate in their minds and in the minds of all humankind to follow, that would rob us of our blessed identity in God.

We often spend days trying to make critical decisions and ages beating ourselves up for incorrect ones. As humans we are consumed by choice. Try to imagine a life where we have freedom of choice and the outcome of any choice we make would always result in good? A world where, because of the correct intent, because of complete trust in God, choices made could never result in harm. A world where we are not bound to make that right choice, but do so because we *want* to. A world where it's our constant and inherent desire to make a Godly choice every time. Because of that one bite of forbidden fruit, we find our lives absolutely consumed by the debate between wrong and right.

Should we or shouldn't we? Must we or must we not? To go or not to go? Stay with him or leave him? Discipline with a spanking or chastise with words? Consume alcohol or not? Methodist or Anglican? Old Testament or New? Post tribulation or pre? Brand name or no-name brand? Private or public school? Sex before or after marriage? Abstinence, ecstasy or acid? Good enough or not? Depressed or happy? And so the debates rage on. Advertising agencies of the world get richer and divorce lawyers rub their hands in financial glee as married partners change their minds and regularly change their spouses. Our motivation to honor God as a living sacrifice and making the right choice has been questioned and in many instances completely replaced by the desire to please self and set self up as the ultimate being to be honored. This is the ultimate battle between the spirit and flesh.

Yes, God has given us free will but what He really wants for us is to have the right motives and inspirations when exercising our freedom of choice. He wants us to put down the selfish motives that were stirred in us by the very first lie and choose to return to the motive of honoring and obeying Him for no other reason than that we trust Him. He has wired into us His qualities and principles. The main wiring box in us is called our conscience.

When we fuel our conscience with His Word and promises, we start making decisions that are focused on honoring Him and not honoring ourselves. Satan is just trying to change our wiring. He wants us to become so focused on ourselves that we forget to honor God by following His way.

THE END OF IT ALL

In Johannesburg, South Africa, a bridge was erected in the city to honor the late Mr. Nelson Mandela. The bridge is named after him and even though there is a more convenient route to the city, people go out of their way to drive over the Nelson Mandela Bridge. By using the roadway across the bridge it gives people a sense that they are honoring Mr. Mandela.

In the same way, we honor God simply by using the principles He has placed in us. By loving our enemies and forgiving those who have hurt us, we honor God. Even though it seems that it is easier to hold onto resentment and harbor a grudge, we dishonor Him by not choosing the forgiveness He has wired into us. As a result we have to live with bitterness and pain.

We don't honor God simply because He tells us too. We honor the principles He has placed in us by making decisions based on them. Our motive is to always discover what He has wired into us and use that wiring to make decisions. His way, His wiring and His principles will always result in the best possible outcome. We can make a whole myriad of choices, but making them based on Him will always work out best. We can be free to make any decision we like; we just need to use His principles.

That was always His purpose. He knows every possible outcome of our decisions and He has a plan for each of them. In the greater scheme of things, it really does not matter if a decision we make ends up with the wrong or right outcome, just as long as we make that decision with His purpose in mind.

And we know that all things work together for good to those who love God, to those who are the called according to His purpose. - Romans 8:28

When we honor God and we love Him back for the love He has bestowed upon us, He will begin showing us the good in every outcome of every decision. He wants us to be motivated by His love which results in trusting and obeying Him. We should never allow believing a lie to take that away from us.

Because God can work for the good in all things, His divine plan cannot be foiled by a poor decision here or a poorly inspired choice there. He is saying to us that if we make decisions with the right motivation, our journeys within that divine plan will be much better. As one who wants us to be with Him forever, He is begging us to listen to His advice. He is crying out to us to please review some of our motives. He is asking us to let Him be our only inspiration and to let that which was lost by Adam and Eve come back into our lives again.

Adam and Eve were instructed by God to fill the earth and subdue it. Their disobedience did not prevent the fulfillment of this plan, just required a different route to achieve it. God has a plan that covers all eventualities and every outcome of the choices we make. In the same way that He had an alternative plan for whatever Adam and Eve's choice might have been, so He has plans for every choice we make and they are plans to prosper us.

For I know the thoughts that I think toward you, says the Lord, thoughts of peace and not of evil, to give you a future and a hope. Jeremiah 29:11

Just as Adam and Eve did, we allow ourselves to doubt God's trustworthiness and the benefit of obedience to Him. We begin to think that we have a better way to handle any situation. We think that perhaps *our* decisions will result in greater benefits for us than the decisions God has recommended we make— ones based on our identity, authority and our purpose.

We have learned that we are created in the same mold as Adam and Eve. God designed them to be blessed. He designed them and as a result designed us to enjoy the blessings of walking with Him and not to become desperate miracle seekers as many of us have.

We cannot forget that God also made Adam and Eve capable of weighing up their choices and making decisions. However, His desire was that they would always trust that the choices He recommended were the best for them, no matter what the immediate outcome may be, whether questions may arise or whether there is an easier option. He wanted them to trust that no matter what choice they made, if it was made in obedience to Him, it would always result in the best possible long term outcome—blessings. He wanted them to desire obedience based completely on the trust they had in His recommendations and His nature. Once trust was in place, obedience would follow naturally and easily and would then unlock the natural consequences of God's blessings. Obedience is not to be motivated by the possible blessings or benefits, but is to be based completely and solely on the trust that we have in our Father's love for us.

God always wants what is best for us. He wants us to make choices that will demonstrate that we trust Him. Trust needs to be proved through action even when it seems as though a solution that God gives us is foolish or contrary to the outcome we desire. God asks us, as He asked Adam and Eve, to simply believe in His way. Once we stop thinking that we may have a better solution and adopt the understanding that no matter how dark things are in the immediate, or how strange what He says seems, God's ways always result in good. The decision to choose God-directed actions then becomes easy.

God's evident love for us should be our motivation to trust Him and once we do, our trust gives birth to our free will obedience. The greater the trust, the greater the obedience and the greater the resultant blessings.

Trust by simple definition is not obedience, but the value we place on trust in God's will relates directly to the value we place on obeying Him. Once God sees our trust motivated obedience, He has promised blessing. He has promised us *happily forever after.* Blessing in our lives now and for all eternity.

That *happily forever after* is something we all long for. We all long to live forever, to know what is on the other side of this life. The idea of an afterlife is built into every human being. I looked back at the studies I had made into many religions and belief structures during my search for "God answers," and I realized that at the heart of all of man's attempts to structure belief and faith, there was an afterlife in each and every one of them.

He has made everything beautiful in its time. **Also He has put eternity in their hearts,** *except that no one can find out the work that God does from beginning to end. - Ecclesiastes 3:11 (emphasis mine)*

We have never seen this eternal future that is seated deep within our psyche. But we still hope for it. This hope that exists in us for eternal life, exists for many other things too. We hope for good things to happen to us and our loved ones, we hope that the plight of the poor will improve and we hope to live happily forever after. Hope is part of who we are. By applying the principle of being made in God's image, we have in us that which exists in God. So, surely then, if we have hope we have received that deep seated hope from God. God is the God of hope! That would explain why we had this hope wired into our DNA.

Hope becomes our fuel. It fuels our faith and as a result it fuels our ability to persevere through the difficult times and rejoice in the good times.

Faith is the confidence that what we hope for will actually happen; it gives us assurance about things we cannot see. Hebrews 11:1

I was afraid of the dark when I was younger. I hated

not knowing what may be out there and not being able to see what was around the corner. Life is like that too. Our default setting when we do not know what will happen is fear. Fear gives birth to worry, stress, depression and anxiety.

Living by God's principles means that we don't have to live with that sense of fear. We can confidently step into the unknown, dive head first into the *things we cannot see* with a confidence that the deeper things we yearn and hope for, wired into us by the God of hope, will actually come to be.

Doing it God's way is not the unknown or the dark that we fear. His word is light and is constant and true. It never fails. The way He has wired us *is* for good. If we are honest with ourselves, deep down we know what He has wired into us, but life has a way of making us deny Him. The more of Him that we deny, the more the fear grows. There is more *unknown* in making decisions based on our own strengths and knowledge than trusting how He has wired us. In the end, doing it our way is actually more foreign than being who He made us to be. Satan has convinced the human race that God's wiring and principles are what should be considered foreign. He has many believing that God is out to dictate to them who they should be and that doing it God's way will rob them of their identity and personality.

Obedience to God is not something that robs us of life, nor does it mean that we give up who we are and what we do. No it means that we get to express who we are and who He has made us to be. He has used difficulties to shape our resolve. He has taken our sadness and turned it into passion. He transforms anger into righteousness and weakness into strength. He always has something good that we can hope in. We have confidence that He wants to give us the life we yearn for because it is He who placed the yearnings in us. Being obedient to Him is not a chore. It is a fulfilling expression of love for Him. Some of us tend to believe that doing it God's way is tedious and that we would have to give up all we are and all we want to become to follow such a heavily principled God.

Many of us translate what God asks us to do to a task list or a set of laws and regulations that we believe will result in the loss of our identity. In fact, however, the things He has asked us to do as believers, matches the desires of our hearts. He wants us to dream of incredible things. He desires us to catch a glimpse of the hope He has and that He placed in us. He wants good things to come from our lives. He does not want us to be clones and robotically obey Him. He loves our individuality and diversity.

He does not want us to be bound up with worry and entrapped by fear. He placed hope in us, gave us His kind of faith, purpose and mission. And once He had wired Himself into us, He also gave us the creative ability to have free will to choose how we would express these incredible fruits in our lives.

But the Holy Spirit produces this kind of fruit in our lives: love, joy, peace, patience, kindness, goodness, faithfulness, gentleness, and self-control. There is no law against these things! - Galatians 5:22-23

I don't know about you, but I hope for and long to have all of nine of those fruits in my life. Law or not, the benefit of obedience to Him far outweighs any so-called "fruit" that this world has to offer.

We must choose. We either make up our own principles and follow those, or we follow the principles God has wired into each and every one of us. Think about it. The reason we have turmoil and anxiety in our lives is because we choose to go our own way in direct contradiction to how God wired us. Fear is nurtured in the space between our will and His will. The greater the gap, the greater the fear.

God desires us to begin choosing to do life His way. He wants the very best for us. Serving God and following His way is not a sacrifice. It is not heavy and complicated. The only sacrifice we need to make is to sacrifice the desire to live our lives according to our ways.

*And so, dear brothers and sisters, I plead with you to give your bodies to God because of all he has done for you. Let them be a **living and holy sacrifice**—the kind he will find acceptable. This is truly the way to worship him. Don't copy the behavior and customs of this world, **but let God transform you into a new person by changing the way you think.** Then you will learn to know God's will for you, which is good and pleasing and perfect. - Romans 12:1-2 (emphasis mine)*

We must change our way of thinking by learning God's will. His will has been wired into us. It is part of who we are. Doing it ourselves is like using a screwdriver as a hammer, not impossible, but difficult. We can get life done choosing to do it our way, but also with great difficulty and with no promise of *happily forever after*.

Get it done with God and what He has wired into you, and it becomes a whole different ball game.

For my yoke is easy and my burden is light. - Matthew 11:30

This is the invitation that Jesus lays before you. It's put like this in <u>The Message</u> by Eugene H. Petersen: "Come to me. Get away with me and you'll recover your life. I'll show you how to take a real rest. Walk with me and work with me—watch how I do it. **Learn the unforced rhythms of grace.** I won't lay anything heavy or ill-fitting on you. Keep company with me and you'll learn to live freely and lightly."

ABOUT THE AUTHOR

Craig was born into a Jehovah's Witness family in Cape Town, South Africa in 1974. He was brought up during the apartheid years in South Africa and was blessed to finally serve his country as it emerged into a new democracy.

With an interesting and varied past that did not always include a personal relationship with Jesus, Craig has a passion for the downtrodden and loves to see Jesus step into situations and radically change lives for the better.

Craig describes his wife Leanne as "his biggest influence and someone who has the most amazing, genuine relationship with God." Leanne serves with Craig in ministry and has, for the last number of years, home schooled their 3 children, Kevin, Bianca and Kyle – all of whom are Christ followers.

In the last 20 years Craig has been used to plant and pastor multiple churches, led at an executive level across Africa and Europe in the telecommunications and banking industries, became a sought after expert in social and digital marketing and communications and became a known international speaker and preacher.

Craig serves as pastor in the United States, heads an international non-profit organization that builds and assists local churches in South Africa and consults with churches globally on strategy and the use of digital communication and social media to connect church and spread the gospel. Find out more at nimble.church.

Made in the USA
Monee, IL
17 August 2021